Vue.js 3 Essentials

Master Reactive UI Development with Composition API, Vue Router, and Vuex

Dennis Rambert

Copyright Page

Table of Contents

Preface 5

Chapter 1: Introduction to Vue.js 3 8

What is Vue.js? 8
Key Features of Vue 3 9
Understanding the Virtual DOM and Reactivity System 11
Differences Between Vue 2 and Vue 3 16
Overview of the Composition API 22
Chapter 2: Setting Up Your Vue 3 Project 27

Installing Vue with Vite 27
Project Structure and Anatomy 31
Using the Vue CLI vs Vite 36
Debugging with Vue DevTools 40
Creating Your First Component 45
Chapter 3: The Essentials of Vue Templates and Reactivity 51

Template Syntax and Directives in Vue 3 51
Data Binding and Interpolation in Vue 3 58
Handling Events and Methods in Vue 3 65
Conditional Rendering and Loops 72
Understanding `ref()` and `reactive()` in Vue 3 79
Chapter 4: Components and Communication 86

Creating Reusable Components 86
Props and Custom Events 93
Understanding Slots in Vue 3 99
Component Lifecycle in Vue 3 107
Start with Intentional Folder Grouping 113
Chapter 5: Composition API Deep Dive 120

What is the `setup()` Function? 120
Creating Reactive Values with `ref()` 127
What Is a Composable? 134
Understanding `provide` and `inject` 140
Mixing Options API with Composition API 147
Chapter 6: Forms and User Input Handling 155

Working with Forms in Vue 155

What is Two-Way Binding? 162

Input Validation 170

Form Validation with Yup 176

Why Use Composition API for Forms 182

Chapter 7: Managing Application State with Vuex 191

What is Vuex ? 191

core concepts of Vuex 196

Modularizing the Vuex Store 204

Vuex and Composition API Integration 211

Managing Auth, Cart, and UI State with Vuex 217

Chapter 8: Navigating with Vue Router 225

Introduction to Vue Router 4 225

Defining Routes, Params, and Query Strings 229

Nested Routes and Route Guards 234

Dynamic Routing and Lazy Loading 241

Navigation Lifecycle and Hooks 247

Chapter 9: Building and Connecting to APIs 254

Fetching Data with Axios and the Fetch API 254

Handling Asynchronous Requests 259

Error Handling and Loading States 266

Building a Reusable API Service 272

Working with REST and GraphQL 277

Chapter 10: Real-World App Development and Deployment 285

Planning the Application Structure 285

Combining Vuex, Router, and Composition API 291

Authentication and Protected Routes 297

Deploying Your App to Netlify, Vercel, or Firebase 305

Performance Optimization and Best Practices 309

Appendices 316

Preface

Vue.js has become a leading framework for building interactive and maintainable web interfaces. With the release of Vue 3, developers now have access to a modernized architecture that includes a more powerful reactivity system, improved performance, and new features such as the Composition API. These updates are designed to support larger-scale applications and improve code organization and reuse.

This book was written to provide a focused and practical approach to learning Vue.js 3. It emphasizes the core concepts that every developer needs to build reliable and scalable applications using modern Vue features. In particular, the book centers on three key areas: the Composition API for managing component logic, Vue Router for client-side navigation, and Vuex for application state management.

Rather than covering everything about Vue, this book concentrates on what is most essential. Each chapter builds on what you've learned in the previous one, with progressively more complex examples and use cases. By the end of the book, you will be equipped to create fully functioning single-page applications using Vue.js 3 and its most important tools.

Who Should Read This Book?

This book is intended for a wide range of developers. If you are new to Vue or frontend development in general, the early chapters provide a solid foundation in reactive programming and component-based architecture. Clear explanations and annotated code samples will help you understand the underlying concepts without requiring prior experience with Vue 2.

If you are already familiar with Vue 2, this book will help you transition to Vue 3 by highlighting key differences and teaching you how to adopt the Composition API and other modern features. Developers coming from other frontend frameworks such as React or Angular will also benefit, as many of the concepts—such as component structure, routing, and state management— are applicable across modern frontend ecosystems.

Backend developers looking to build dynamic frontend interfaces will find that Vue 3 offers a manageable learning curve and integrates easily with RESTful

APIs and common deployment platforms. The code examples are written in JavaScript, but knowledge of TypeScript is not required to follow along.

How to Use This Book

This book is designed to be read in order from beginning to end. Each chapter introduces new concepts and builds upon the material from previous chapters. However, developers with experience in some areas may choose to skip directly to specific chapters, such as the ones on Vuex or Vue Router.

Each concept is explained in plain terms before being demonstrated in code. You are encouraged to read the explanations carefully, review the code samples, and then implement the examples on your own. The book provides numerous opportunities to reinforce what you've learned through practical exercises and mini-projects.

Where appropriate, the book introduces recommended libraries and tools that enhance the Vue development experience. You will learn how to work with these tools in a practical context, rather than as separate theoretical topics.

Tools and Requirements

To follow the examples in this book, you will need a computer with an internet connection and the ability to install software. The development environment is based on modern tooling:

Node.js: A JavaScript runtime used to install packages and run development servers.

npm or Yarn: Package managers used to manage dependencies.

Vite: A fast build tool and development server recommended for Vue 3 projects.

Vue DevTools: A browser extension that helps inspect and debug Vue components and their state.

Basic familiarity with JavaScript is assumed. If you are new to JavaScript, you may want to review key topics such as variables, functions, arrays, objects, and asynchronous programming with `async/await`.

All code samples are written in standard JavaScript (ES6 and above), and care has been taken to explain any syntax that may be unfamiliar. You do not need prior experience with build tools or modern JavaScript frameworks to benefit from this book.

All source code used in this book is available in a public GitHub repository. Each chapter includes links to specific folders or files so you can see the complete, working version of every example. Instructions for cloning the repository and running the code on your machine are provided in the first chapter.

You are encouraged to experiment with the code—modify it, break it, and fix it. Active experimentation is one of the most effective ways to understand how Vue's reactivity system, component architecture, and supporting libraries work in real scenarios.

As updates to Vue and its ecosystem are released, the repository will also include version notes and possible updates to ensure the material remains relevant and compatible with future versions.

Chapter 1: Introduction to Vue.js 3

Before we start building anything with Vue, let's take a step back and understand what Vue is, why it has become so popular, and what makes Vue 3 such a significant update in the framework's evolution. Whether you're brand new to frontend development or transitioning from another framework like React or Angular, this chapter is here to give you the context you need.

What is Vue.js?

Vue.js is a **JavaScript framework** used to build **user interfaces** (UIs) and **single-page applications** (SPAs). It allows developers to create interactive, data-driven web applications with a focus on simplicity, clarity, and maintainability.

At its core, Vue is designed to be **declarative**. This means instead of writing step-by-step instructions to manipulate the user interface, you describe what the interface should look like based on the current application state. Vue automatically updates the interface when the state changes. This results in less code and fewer bugs because you don't need to manually manage updates to the DOM (Document Object Model).

Vue is often referred to as a **progressive framework**, which means you can use as little or as much of it as you need. For example, you can include Vue in a single HTML page to add interactivity to a specific part of your site. But if your project grows, Vue can scale with it—supporting components, routing, state management, and build tools. This makes it suitable for both small enhancements and full-featured applications.

One of Vue's defining features is its **component-based architecture**. A component is a reusable block of code that includes the HTML, CSS, and JavaScript needed to display and control a part of your interface—such as a button, form input, or navigation bar. Components can be composed together to form larger and more complex interfaces. This approach improves modularity and makes it easier to maintain code over time.

Another key concept in Vue is **reactivity**. Vue uses a reactive data system that automatically tracks dependencies between data and the user interface. When your data changes, Vue knows exactly which parts of the DOM depend on that data and updates them efficiently. You don't need to write custom logic to watch for changes or re-render the interface manually.

Vue's syntax and API are designed to be **approachable** for developers coming from HTML, CSS, and JavaScript backgrounds. It uses a combination of familiar HTML templates and JavaScript logic, which helps reduce the learning curve compared to more complex frameworks. For example, rendering a list, binding user input, or conditionally displaying elements can be done using intuitive and readable syntax.

While Vue shares some concepts with other frameworks like React and Angular, it distinguishes itself with a lightweight core, sensible defaults, and flexibility. Developers are not forced into a single way of working. Vue offers structure when needed but also leaves room for customization.

In practical terms, Vue helps developers build applications that are faster, more responsive, and easier to maintain. Whether you are creating a simple feature or a large application, Vue provides the tools to structure your code, manage user interactions, and keep your interface in sync with your data.

As we move through this book, you'll learn how Vue builds on these principles through features like the Composition API, Vue Router, and Vuex—all of which make it a modern and powerful solution for building interactive web applications.

Key Features of Vue 3

Vue 3 introduces several improvements and new capabilities that make the framework more powerful, efficient, and flexible compared to previous versions. While the overall philosophy of Vue remains the same—focused on simplicity and ease of use—Vue 3 modernizes the framework to better support larger applications, improve performance, and provide a more consistent developer experience.

One of the most significant updates in Vue 3 is the introduction of the **Composition API**. This is a new way to organize logic inside components. In Vue 2, the default approach is the Options API, where you define your data, methods, computed properties, and lifecycle hooks in separate sections of a component. While this works well for small components, it can become harder to manage as components grow in complexity. The Composition API allows you to group related logic together within a single `setup()` function. This makes the code more modular and easier to reuse across different components.

Another important improvement is **enhanced performance**. Vue 3 is faster than Vue 2 in several key areas, including rendering, memory usage, and component initialization. These performance gains come from a complete rewrite of the core using a more efficient architecture. As a result, applications built with Vue 3 can handle more complex interfaces with less processing overhead.

Vue 3 is also built with **TypeScript** at its foundation. Although you don't need to write TypeScript to use Vue 3, the framework's internal codebase is now fully written in TypeScript. This change improves editor support, static analysis, and type safety. For developers who do use TypeScript, Vue 3 provides better tooling and more consistent type definitions.

Support for **multiple root elements** in a single component is another feature introduced in Vue 3. In Vue 2, a component template was required to have exactly one root element, which sometimes led to unnecessary wrapper elements in the DOM. Vue 3 removes this limitation, allowing components to return fragments—multiple top-level elements—which results in cleaner and more semantic markup.

Vue 3 also includes new built-in components such as **Teleport** and **Suspense**. Teleport allows you to render a piece of a component's template in a different part of the DOM. This is especially useful for modals, tooltips, or notifications that need to appear outside their parent component's layout structure. Suspense provides a way to handle asynchronous components more gracefully by showing fallback content while a component is loading. These features make it easier to manage dynamic UI behaviors in a more declarative and controlled manner.

Another improvement is **better support for large-scale application development**. Vue 3 has been designed with scalability in mind. It supports tree-shaking, which allows build tools to exclude unused parts of the framework from the final bundle. This leads to smaller file sizes and faster load times. Combined with Vite, a fast build tool recommended for Vue 3 projects, developers can enjoy near-instant development feedback and efficient production builds.

The **reactivity system** in Vue 3 has also been rewritten to be more flexible and precise. It now uses a mechanism based on ES6 Proxies instead of the `Object.defineProperty` method used in Vue 2. This change allows Vue to track changes to more complex data structures like arrays and nested objects more reliably. It also makes the internal dependency tracking system more efficient, leading to fewer unnecessary updates in the DOM.

Together, these features make Vue 3 a significant step forward. It retains the simplicity and readability that Vue is known for, while offering the tools needed to build high-performance, maintainable, and scalable applications. Whether you're creating a simple component or managing a complex application with many moving parts, Vue 3 provides the structure and flexibility needed to support modern frontend development.

Understanding the Virtual DOM and Reactivity System

To build efficient and dynamic web applications, it's important to understand not just what Vue does, but how it does it. Two of the most important ideas that make Vue 3 powerful are its **Virtual DOM** and its **reactivity system**. Together, these form the foundation of how Vue responds to user input, tracks data, and keeps your interface synchronized with your application state.

What Is the Virtual DOM in Vue?

Every web page is made up of a structure called the **Document Object Model**, or DOM. The DOM represents the HTML content of a web page in a tree-like format. You can think of it as the browser's internal model of the page structure. Whenever JavaScript manipulates elements—changing the text in a paragraph, hiding a modal, updating a list—the DOM has to be updated. These updates are often expensive, especially when they happen frequently or on large sections of the page.

To avoid repeatedly changing the DOM directly, Vue 3 uses something called the **Virtual DOM**. This is a lightweight JavaScript-based copy of the real DOM. When the state of your application changes, Vue doesn't immediately touch the actual DOM. Instead, it updates this virtual copy first. Vue then compares the updated virtual DOM to the previous one using a process called **diffing**, and it figures out exactly what has changed. It applies only those minimal changes to the real DOM, and nothing more.

This makes updates faster and more efficient. It's the same strategy used in frameworks like React, but Vue's implementation is optimized for both speed and memory efficiency.

Let's walk through a simple example.

```
<template>
  <div>
    <p>{{ message }}</p>
    <button @click="changeMessage">Change
Message</button>
  </div>
</template>

<script>
import { ref } from 'vue'

export default {
  setup() {
    const message = ref('Hello, Vue!')

    function changeMessage() {
      message.value = 'Vue has changed me!'
    }

    return {
      message,
      changeMessage
    }
  }
}
</script>
```

In this component, you're displaying a paragraph with some text, and you provide a button to update that text. When the button is clicked, Vue updates the `message` value. Internally, Vue doesn't go and re-render the entire page. It updates the virtual DOM, sees that only the text inside the `<p>` element has changed, and only patches that specific part of the actual DOM. Everything else remains untouched.

This is why Vue apps feel fast and responsive, even when they handle many dynamic updates. The framework is minimizing the cost of DOM operations without you having to manually track or optimize anything.

How Vue's Reactivity System Works

Now that you understand the role of the Virtual DOM, the next piece is understanding how Vue knows **when** to update it. This is where reactivity comes into play.

In Vue 3, the reactivity system has been completely rewritten using a feature in modern JavaScript called **Proxies**. A Proxy allows Vue to intercept interactions with an object—like reading a property or updating a value—and automatically track those changes.

Here's the core idea: when you define reactive data in Vue, the framework wraps it in a special structure that allows it to watch for changes. When you access or modify that data, Vue tracks the dependency and knows which parts of your interface need to respond to that change.

Take this basic use of `ref()` and `reactive()` in Vue 3:

```
import { ref, reactive } from 'vue'

export default {
  setup() {
    const count = ref(0) // a single primitive value
    const user = reactive({
      name: 'Sarah',
      age: 28
    }) // a reactive object with multiple properties
```

```
    function increment() {
        count.value++
        user.age++
    }

    return {
        count,
        user,
        increment
    }
  }
}
```

In this component, `count` is a reactive reference to a number, and `user` is a reactive object. When `increment()` is called, Vue tracks the fact that `count.value` and `user.age` were modified. Any part of your component template that depends on these values will be automatically updated without you writing any additional code.

This is what makes Vue a **reactive framework**: it reacts automatically when your data changes.

Unlike Vue 2, which used `Object.defineProperty()` to intercept property access and mutation, Vue 3's Proxy-based system has several key advantages. It can observe changes to **newly added properties**, handle **arrays and nested objects** more accurately, and track **delete operations**—all of which were either not possible or required workarounds in Vue 2.

How Vue Tracks Dependencies

One question developers often ask is how Vue knows which parts of the interface depend on which pieces of data. The answer is dependency tracking.

When a component renders, Vue "collects" any reactive values used during the rendering process. It remembers which reactive data points are being accessed, and it links them to the functions that need to re-run when those values change.

These functions are called **effects**, and Vue registers them automatically during rendering. When a reactive value changes, Vue re-runs the relevant effects and updates the Virtual DOM, which then leads to updates in the real DOM.

You don't need to manage these effects directly. Vue handles it for you behind the scenes, but the understanding is helpful when designing components that depend on a lot of dynamic data.

Practical Exercise: Live Character Counter

Let's write a small component that makes good use of both the reactivity system and efficient DOM updates.

```
<template>
  <div>
    <label for="bio">Your Bio:</label>
    <textarea id="bio" v-model="bio"></textarea>
    <p>Character count: {{ characterCount }}</p>
  </div>
</template>

<script>
import { ref, computed } from 'vue'

export default {
  setup() {
    const bio = ref('')

    const characterCount = computed(() =>
bio.value.length)

    return {
      bio,
      characterCount
    }
  }
}
</script>
```

Here, the user can type into a textarea. The `bio` variable is reactive because it was created with `ref()`. The `characterCount` is computed based on `bio`, and will automatically update when `bio.value` changes. Vue tracks the relationship between `bio` and `characterCount`, and it updates the DOM precisely and only when needed.

No manual event listeners. No direct DOM manipulation. Just reactive state and automatic updates.

How This Applies in Real Applications

Think about a product page in an online store. When a user selects a different product option, like color or size, the price, stock availability, and preview image might all change. With Vue's reactivity system in place, these changes can be wired directly to the reactive state that manages selected options. Vue ensures that all relevant parts of the UI update together—without forcing the developer to manually track which DOM elements need to change or when.

This saves time, reduces bugs, and leads to cleaner, more maintainable code.

Understanding the Virtual DOM and Vue's reactivity system is fundamental to using the framework effectively. Vue's Virtual DOM ensures updates are applied efficiently by making changes in memory first and applying only what's necessary to the real DOM. The reactivity system tracks which parts of the UI depend on which pieces of data, and it updates them automatically when the data changes.

This combination is what gives Vue its responsiveness and ease of development. As you continue building more interactive components, you'll start to see how these core systems do a lot of the heavy lifting, allowing you to focus on logic and design rather than DOM manipulation or performance tuning.

Differences Between Vue 2 and Vue 3

If you've spent time working with Vue 2, or even just reviewed some of its documentation, you'll notice that many things feel familiar in Vue 3. The core philosophy of reactive components, declarative templates, and component-based architecture remains the same. However, under the surface—and in several key areas above the surface—Vue 3 introduces meaningful changes that affect how you write, structure, and scale applications.

One of the most significant differences is how logic is organized inside components. Vue 2 uses what's called the **Options API**. In this approach, when you write a component, you organize your logic by option types: data goes in the data() method, functions go under methods, computed properties are declared in computed, and lifecycle hooks like mounted() and created() live in their own sections. While this structure is easy to understand for small components, it becomes harder to manage when your component grows. Related logic is split into multiple sections of the file, making it harder to understand and reuse.

Vue 3 introduces the **Composition API** to solve this. Instead of splitting code by option type, you group related functionality together inside a setup() function. This allows you to extract and reuse logic more easily, and it also makes complex components more maintainable. The Composition API is especially helpful when you need to share logic across components— something that required mixins or scoped slots in Vue 2, which often came with their own limitations like naming conflicts and unclear origins of data.

Let's compare both styles using a real example. Suppose you're building a component that tracks a mouse position and responds to it.

Vue 2 with Options API:

```
export default {
  data() {
    return {
      x: 0,
      y: 0
    }
  },
  mounted() {
    window.addEventListener('mousemove',
this.updateMouse)
  },
  beforeUnmount() {
    window.removeEventListener('mousemove',
this.updateMouse)
  },
  methods: {
    updateMouse(event) {
      this.x = event.clientX
```

```
      this.y = event.clientY
    }
  }
}
```

Vue 3 with Composition API:

```
import { ref, onMounted, onBeforeUnmount } from
'vue'

export default {
  setup() {
    const x = ref(0)
    const y = ref(0)

    function updateMouse(event) {
      x.value = event.clientX
      y.value = event.clientY
    }

    onMounted(() => {
      window.addEventListener('mousemove',
updateMouse)
    })

    onBeforeUnmount(() => {
      window.removeEventListener('mousemove',
updateMouse)
    })

    return {
      x,
      y
    }
  }
}
```

Both examples do the same thing, but notice how the Vue 3 version keeps everything together. The reactive state (x and y), the event handler (updateMouse), and the lifecycle hooks are all grouped in the same place. This structure becomes especially valuable as components become more complex, because it improves clarity and makes logic easier to extract into reusable functions, often referred to as *composables*.

Another important difference is in how Vue handles reactivity under the hood. Vue 2 uses `Object.defineProperty` to convert plain objects into reactive ones. This works for the most part, but it has limitations. For example, Vue 2 cannot detect when new properties are added to an object after it's been made reactive. It also struggles with reactivity in arrays, particularly when using methods like `splice()` or `sort()`.

Vue 3 replaces that system with one based on **ES6 Proxies**. A proxy in JavaScript allows you to define custom behavior for fundamental operations like getting or setting a property. With proxies, Vue 3 can track changes to any property—including properties that are added later—and it can also better observe array operations. This makes the reactivity system in Vue 3 more accurate, reliable, and flexible, especially when working with complex or deeply nested data structures.

This change also affects how you declare reactive state. In Vue 2, you typically define data inside a `data()` method that returns an object. In Vue 3, you use functions like `ref()` for primitive values and `reactive()` for objects.

Here's a simple example of the difference:

Vue 2:

```
export default {
  data() {
    return {
      count: 0
    }
  }
}
```

Vue 3:

```
import { ref } from 'vue'

export default {
  setup() {
    const count = ref(0)

    return {
      count
    }
```

```
    }
  }
```

Both approaches result in a reactive `count` variable that can be used in the template, but Vue 3's `ref()` is more explicit and gives you fine-grained control over how reactivity works. When accessing a `ref`, you use `.value` in JavaScript, though Vue handles this automatically inside templates.

Another area where Vue 3 differs is in its support for **TypeScript**. While Vue 2 had some support for TypeScript, it was limited and often difficult to use effectively. Vue 3 was rewritten in TypeScript from the ground up. This doesn't mean you need to use TypeScript in your own projects, but it does mean you get better type inference, IDE support, and integration if you choose to do so. For teams building large applications or using strict typing, this change provides stronger tooling and improved maintainability.

The component model in Vue 3 has also been updated to support **multiple root nodes** in a template. In Vue 2, each component's template was required to return exactly one root element. This sometimes forced developers to wrap content in unnecessary `<div>` tags, just to satisfy the requirement. Vue 3 removes that restriction. Now, you can return multiple root elements from a single component without any issues. This results in cleaner and more semantic markup.

For example:

Vue 2:

```
<template>
  <div>
    <header>Header</header>
    <main>Main content</main>
    <footer>Footer</footer>
  </div>
</template>
```

Vue 3:

```
<template>
  <header>Header</header>
  <main>Main content</main>
  <footer>Footer</footer>
```

```
</template>
```

This change is small in appearance but significant in practice, especially when designing layout components or working with native HTML structure that doesn't naturally fit into a single wrapper.

Finally, Vue 3 includes two new built-in components: `Teleport` and `Suspense`. These provide solutions to common challenges in modern frontend development. `Teleport` lets you render part of your component tree somewhere else in the DOM. It's useful for modals, tooltips, and other UI elements that need to appear outside their logical parent for layout reasons. `Suspense` provides a structured way to handle asynchronous components. When loading data or fetching code-split components, you can use `Suspense` to display fallback content until everything is ready, giving your users a smoother experience.

These new components reflect a broader trend in Vue 3's design: adding features that developers often built workarounds for in Vue 2, and turning them into first-class features of the framework.

To bring all of this into a practical context, consider a large-scale application like an admin dashboard for an e-commerce platform. In Vue 2, managing shared logic across multiple complex components often involved patterns like mixins, which could become difficult to trace and debug. In Vue 3, the Composition API enables reusable, testable logic that can be organized in separate files, improving both scalability and maintainability. Vue 3's improved reactivity ensures that deeply nested data structures, such as user profiles, order records, and real-time analytics, are updated efficiently and correctly, even as the complexity grows.

These differences are not just technical—they have a real impact on how you write and maintain Vue applications. Vue 3 gives you more control, better tooling, and performance benefits that matter at both small and large scales. As you work through this book, you'll use these improvements in practice and gain the confidence to adopt Vue 3 for both new and existing projects.

Overview of the Composition API

If you've already written a few components using the Options API in Vue 2 or even Vue 3, you've likely seen the familiar structure: `data`, `methods`, `computed`, and lifecycle hooks like `mounted` all living in clearly named sections. While this structure works well for small or straightforward components, it begins to create challenges as the logic becomes more complex.

When a component grows large, related pieces of functionality often end up separated into different sections of the file. You might have a form where the validation logic is in `methods`, the form state is in `data`, and your computed validations live in `computed`. Even though they all relate to the same task, they're scattered across the component. This makes the code harder to read and even harder to reuse.

Vue 3 introduces the **Composition API** as a way to solve this exact problem.

Rather than organizing your component by *option type*, the Composition API allows you to organize it by *logical concern*. This means all the code related to a specific feature—say, form input handling or API data fetching—can be grouped together, making the component more readable and modular.

The key to using the Composition API is the `setup()` function. This function is called before the component is created, and it's where you define your reactive state, computed properties, functions, watchers, and more. Anything returned from the `setup()` function becomes available for use in the component's template.

Let's start with a simple example to demonstrate how it works.

Here's a basic counter component using the Composition API:

```
<template>
  <div>
    <p>Count: {{ count }}</p>
    <button @click="increment">Increment</button>
  </div>
</template>
```

```
<script>
import { ref } from 'vue'

export default {
  setup() {
    const count = ref(0)

    const increment = () => {
      count.value++
    }

    return {
      count,
      increment
    }
  }
}
</script>
```

Let's break this down carefully.

Inside the `setup()` function, we're using a function called `ref()`. This is part of Vue's reactivity system. `ref()` creates a reactive reference to a value. In this case, we're initializing `count` with a value of `0`. Unlike plain variables, a `ref` allows Vue to track changes to that value and update the DOM accordingly. When `count.value` changes, the component automatically re-renders the part of the template that displays the count.

You'll notice we use `.value` to access or change the contents of a `ref`. This is required when you're working in JavaScript. However, inside the template, Vue handles this automatically, so you don't need to use `.value` in your HTML.

The `increment()` function simply increases `count.value` by one. We return both `count` and `increment` from `setup()` so that they can be used in the template. Anything you return from `setup()` becomes part of the component's context and can be used directly in the template, just like properties declared with the Options API.

This structure might seem like more code at first, but the benefits become clear as you add more logic.

Let's extend this example into something a little more realistic—a component that handles user input and performs validation.

```
<template>
  <div>
    <label for="email">Email:</label>
    <input id="email" v-model="email" />
    <p v-if="!isValidEmail">Please enter a valid
email address.</p>
    <button
:disabled="!isValidEmail">Submit</button>
  </div>
</template>

<script>
import { ref, computed } from 'vue'

export default {
  setup() {
    const email = ref('')

    const isValidEmail = computed(() => {
      return
/^[^\s@]+@[^\s@]+\.[^\s@]+$/.test(email.value)
    })

    return {
      email,
      isValidEmail
    }
  }
}
</script>
```

This example introduces a new function from the Composition API: `computed()`. Just like in the Options API, a computed property automatically tracks any reactive values it depends on and re-evaluates when they change. Here, `isValidEmail` will update every time the user types in the input, and

Vue will automatically show or hide the validation message and enable or disable the button based on that state.

Again, this structure keeps all the related logic—email input and validation—together in the `setup()` function. There's no need to separate `data`, `computed`, and `methods`. The code is easier to follow and easier to extract into reusable utilities if needed.

Now let's take it a step further and extract that email validation logic into a **composable function**. A composable is simply a regular JavaScript function that uses Vue's Composition API features and returns reactive state or behavior. Composables are useful when you want to reuse logic across components.

Here's how you might write a `useEmailValidation.js` composable:

```js
// useEmailValidation.js
import { ref, computed } from 'vue'

export function useEmailValidation() {
  const email = ref('')

  const isValid = computed(() => {
    return
/^[^\s@]+@[^\s@]+\.[^\s@]+$/.test(email.value)
  })

  return {
    email,
    isValid
  }
}
```

Now, in your component, you can use it like this:

```js
<script>
import { useEmailValidation } from
'./useEmailValidation.js'

export default {
  setup() {
    const { email, isValid } = useEmailValidation()
```

```
    return {
      email,
      isValid
    }
  }
}
</script>
```

This kind of modular design wasn't easily achievable with Vue 2. You would have needed to use mixins or scoped slots, both of which had drawbacks like naming conflicts and tight coupling to component structure. With the Composition API, you're writing plain JavaScript functions, which means you can use standard programming techniques to share and organize code.

Another advantage of the Composition API is its support for **TypeScript**, which is now much more robust in Vue 3. Because you're writing pure functions with explicit return values, TypeScript can infer types more accurately. Even if you're not using TypeScript yet, this makes the API design cleaner and more predictable.

As your components grow to include things like timers, watchers, API calls, or lifecycle hooks, you'll find the Composition API gives you the ability to group logic by feature rather than by syntax type. This leads to code that's easier to understand, maintain, and test.

You can still use the Options API in Vue 3, and it remains fully supported. In fact, you can mix both styles in the same project if needed. However, when you're building larger features or want to organize reusable code more effectively, the Composition API provides a clearer path forward.

As an exercise, try building a simple contact form using `ref()` for reactive inputs, `computed()` for validation, and extract any repeated logic into a composable. This will help you understand not just how to use the Composition API, but why it makes certain patterns more practical and scalable.

This isn't just a new syntax—it's a new approach to designing components that scales better as your application grows.

Chapter 2: Setting Up Your Vue 3 Project

Before we start building with Vue 3, we need to set up a development environment that gives us the right tools and structure for building modern, fast, and maintainable applications. Vue is incredibly flexible—you can start with just a script tag in an HTML file, but for anything more than a quick demo, you'll want to use a build tool that supports component-based architecture, hot module replacement, fast reloads, and modular file organization.

That's where **Vite** comes in. In this chapter, we'll walk through installing Vue with Vite, understanding how your project is structured, comparing Vite and Vue CLI, and using Vue DevTools for debugging. We'll wrap up by creating your first Vue 3 component using the Composition API.

Installing Vue with Vite

Before you can build anything with Vue 3, the first thing you need is a proper development environment. In modern frontend development, that means working with a **build tool**—a system that takes your Vue components, JavaScript modules, CSS files, and assets and compiles them into a format the browser can run efficiently.

In the Vue ecosystem today, the recommended tool for this job is **Vite**.

Vite was developed by the creator of Vue, Evan You, specifically to provide a faster and more efficient experience for Vue developers. The name "Vite" is derived from the French word for "fast," and that's exactly what it's built to be. It uses native ES modules in the browser for instant startup and fast hot module replacement (HMR), which means when you save a file, your browser updates immediately—without a full page reload.

Let's walk step-by-step through the process of installing Vue 3 using Vite, so you can get started with a clean and modern development setup.

Step 1: Verify Node.js Installation

First, make sure you have **Node.js** installed. Vite depends on Node.js to install and run project dependencies. You can check your current Node version by opening a terminal and typing:

```
node -v
```

You should see something like `v18.17.0` or newer. If your version is lower than 16, or if you get an error saying `node` is not recognized, then you'll need to download and install the latest Long-Term Support (LTS) version from the official website:

https://nodejs.org

Once installed, restart your terminal and confirm that Node is now available by re-running the version check.

Step 2: Create a New Vue 3 Project with Vite

With Node installed, you can now scaffold a new Vue 3 project using the official Vite project generator. This tool will guide you through creating the initial structure of your application with minimal effort.

Open your terminal and run:

```
npm create vite@latest
```

This command will launch an interactive prompt asking for the name of your project folder. Let's call it `my-vue-app` for now. After you type the name and press enter, Vite will then ask you to select a framework.

When prompted:

```
Select a framework:
> vue
```

Choose `vue` from the list using your arrow keys and press enter.

Now Vite will scaffold your project files into a new folder called `my-vue-app`.

Step 3: Navigate into Your Project and Install Dependencies

Once Vite has generated your project structure, go into your new project folder:

```
cd my-vue-app
```

Then install all required project dependencies using:

28

```
npm install
```
This step uses the `package.json` file that was created during scaffolding to download everything your Vue app needs to run in development. You'll see output in the terminal as Vite installs Vue, development tools, and scripts to run your app locally.

Step 4: Start the Development Server

Now that everything is installed, you can launch the app:

```
npm run dev
```
This command starts the Vite development server. If everything went correctly, the terminal should output something like:

```
VITE v5.0.0  ready in 300 ms

➜  Local:   http://localhost:5173/
```

Open the URL in your browser. You should see a basic welcome screen saying:

```
You did it!
Vite + Vue
```

This means your Vue 3 project is up and running, powered by Vite, and ready for development.

Understanding What Just Happened

Let's stop for a moment to look at what you now have. You didn't just download Vue—you scaffolded a fully functional Vue 3 application, complete with:

A local development server that automatically reloads when you save your files.

A modern module system using ES modules (no bundling during development).

Hot Module Replacement, meaning changes appear instantly in the browser without a full page refresh.

A file structure that's ready to scale as your application grows.

This kind of setup used to take hours of manual configuration with older tools like Webpack. With Vite, it happens in minutes.

Practical Exercise: Customize the Welcome Screen

Now that your app is running, try customizing the homepage to get a feel for how live updates work with Vite.

Open the project in your code editor (such as VS Code), and navigate to:

`src/App.vue`

Inside this file, you'll see a combination of template markup and script logic. Locate the line that says:

```
<h1>Vite + Vue</h1>
```
Change it to something like:

```
<h1>My First Vue 3 App with Vite</h1>
```
Save the file. If your development server is still running, your browser should update instantly—without a refresh. This is Vite's hot module replacement in action, making frontend development feel as responsive as editing a static HTML file.

This feedback loop—write code, save, and see the result immediately—is a big part of why Vite makes Vue development more productive and enjoyable.

Why Vite Matters in Real Projects

In real-world applications, especially those that grow in size and complexity, fast rebuild times and developer feedback loops make a huge difference. Vite was built to solve problems Vue developers often faced with older tools:

Waiting too long for the app to start after every change.

Complex configuration files just to set up a basic project.

Inefficient rebuilds that slowed down productivity as your codebase grew.

Vite is designed to avoid all of that by serving source files directly to the browser using native modules during development, and compiling the optimized version only when you're ready to build for production.

It also works extremely well with Vue's modern features, including the Composition API, Vue Router, and Vuex or Pinia. As a result, you spend less time configuring tools and more time building features.

By installing Vue with Vite, you've taken the first step toward modern Vue 3 development. You've not only scaffolded a project but also equipped yourself with a fast, reliable toolchain that works seamlessly with Vue's latest features.

Project Structure and Anatomy

When you create a new Vue 3 project using Vite, you're given a project structure that's minimal but fully functional. It includes everything you need to start building right away, without overloading you with unnecessary configuration. Every file and folder serves a clear purpose, and understanding them early on will help you write better organized, maintainable code.

Let's explore what you'll see inside the project folder after running `npm create vite@latest` and choosing the Vue template.

Here's what the top level of your project looks like:

```
my-vue-app/
├── node_modules/
├── public/
├── src/
├── .gitignore
├── index.html
├── package.json
├── vite.config.js
```

Each of these files and folders plays a specific role in the development and build process.

Your Source Code Lives in `src/`

This is the most important folder in the entire project. It's where you'll spend nearly all your time writing Vue components, managing application logic, styling your app, and organizing features. Let's walk through the main parts of it.

When you open `src/`, you'll typically find:

```
src/
├── assets/
├── components/
├── App.vue
├── main.js
```

The `assets/` folder is where you can place images, fonts, and any other static files that need to be imported into your components. For example, if you have a logo that you want to use in your header, this is where you'd put it. You can then import it in a component like this:

```
<script setup>
import logo from '../assets/logo.png'
</script>

<template>
  <img :src="logo" alt="App Logo" />
</template>
```

The `components/` folder is where you'll store all your Vue components. A component is a reusable piece of your user interface, such as a header, button, form, or layout element. Keeping them in this folder helps maintain separation of concerns, especially as your app grows.

For example, let's say you want to create a `UserCard.vue` component. You'd create a new file inside `components/` and define it like this:

```
<template>
  <div class="user-card">
    <h2>{{ name }}</h2>
    <p>Email: {{ email }}</p>
  </div>
```

```
</template>

<script setup>
defineProps({
  name: String,
  email: String
})
</script>

<style scoped>
.user-card {
  border: 1px solid #ccc;
  padding: 1rem;
  border-radius: 5px;
}
</style>
```

You can then import and use this component in App.vue or any other parent component.

App.vue is your root component. This is the starting point for your app's component tree. All other components eventually connect to this one, either directly or indirectly. When your app is loaded in the browser, App.vue is the first component Vue renders.

Inside App.vue, you'll usually define your global layout—things like the header, footer, or side menu that wrap your individual pages or features. You can also use it to include components like a navigation bar or your main application container.

Then there's main.js. This is the **entry point** for your app. It's where Vue creates your application instance, tells it what the root component is, and mounts everything to the page. This file usually looks something like this in a brand new project:

```
import { createApp } from 'vue'
import App from './App.vue'

createApp(App).mount('#app')
```

This short snippet is doing a lot. It tells Vue: "Create a new app using the `App.vue` component as the root, and mount it to the HTML element with the ID `app`."

Speaking of that HTML element—let's look at where it comes from.

The Role of `index.html`

Unlike Vue CLI, where `index.html` is hidden inside the `public` folder and managed by Webpack, Vite uses the `index.html` file right at the root of your project.

This file is served directly during development and processed during production builds. It contains the basic structure of your web page and defines where your Vue app will be injected.

If you open `index.html`, you'll see this:

```
<!DOCTYPE html>
<html lang="en">
  <head>
    <meta charset="UTF-8" />
    <link rel="icon" href="/favicon.ico" />
    <meta name="viewport" content="width=device-
width, initial-scale=1.0" />
    <title>Vite + Vue</title>
  </head>
  <body>
    <div id="app"></div>
    <script type="module"
src="/src/main.js"></script>
  </body>
</html>
```

The `<div id="app"></div>` is where your Vue component tree starts rendering—this matches the ID passed to `.mount('#app')` in your `main.js`.

The `<script type="module">` line points to your entry file (`main.js`) and tells the browser to load it using modern ES module syntax, which is part of why Vite can be so fast.

34

The `public/` Folder

Files in the `public/` folder are served directly to the browser **as-is**. That means they're not processed by Vite or included in your dependency graph. You typically use this folder for assets that don't need to be imported into your JavaScript code—like a `robots.txt` file or a custom favicon.

For example, if you put an image called `banner.jpg` in `public/`, it will be accessible at `http://localhost:5173/banner.jpg`.

This is useful when working with static files that aren't part of the component logic but still need to be available to the browser.

Configuration and Dependency Files

Let's talk briefly about a few more important files at the root of your project.

The `package.json` file manages your dependencies, scripts, and project metadata. When you run `npm install`, it installs the packages listed in this file. When you run `npm run dev`, it uses the scripts defined here to start your development server. You'll rarely need to touch this file unless you're adding dependencies or customizing your scripts.

The `vite.config.js` file is where you can customize Vite's behavior. For example, you can define path aliases, add plugins, configure build options, and more. If you want to create a shorthand alias for importing components, you might do something like this:

```
import { defineConfig } from 'vite'
import vue from '@vitejs/plugin-vue'
import path from 'path'

export default defineConfig({
  plugins: [vue()],
  resolve: {
    alias: {
      '@': path.resolve(__dirname, './src')
    }
  }
})
```

With this config, you can now import files like this:

35

```
import MyComponent from '@/components/MyComponent.vue'
```

Instead of using long relative paths like
`../../../components/MyComponent.vue`.

Let's say you're working on a small product listing application. You would store your reusable UI elements—like `ProductCard.vue` or `AddToCartButton.vue`—inside `src/components/`. You might create a new folder like `src/views/` to hold top-level screens like `ProductList.vue` and `ProductDetails.vue`. Your shared utilities could live in `src/utils/`, and Vuex or Pinia store modules in `src/store/`.

This kind of structure keeps things modular and easy to reason about. Each folder and file has a clear purpose. As your app grows, maintaining this structure becomes even more important for keeping your code readable, organized, and easy to test.

Your Vue 3 project structure is more than just a collection of folders—it reflects how your app is organized, how responsibilities are separated, and how easily you can navigate and scale your codebase. By understanding where things belong and why, you'll write cleaner code, make fewer mistakes, and feel more confident as you develop.

You now know how the `src/`, `public/`, `index.html`, and configuration files all work together to support the application. You also know how components are created, how they fit into the `App.vue` root, and how `main.js` ties it all together.

Using the Vue CLI vs Vite

If you've worked with Vue before Vue 3 became mainstream, chances are you've used **Vue CLI**. For a long time, Vue CLI was the official tool for scaffolding and building Vue applications. It provided a standard way to create projects, install plugins, and build your app for development and production. That said, Vue CLI is no longer the recommended tool for new Vue 3 projects—and understanding why starts with understanding how these tools work under the hood.

Let's start with Vue CLI.

Vue CLI is built on **Webpack**, which is a powerful and flexible module bundler. When you run `vue create`, Vue CLI generates a project and sets up Webpack configurations to bundle your source code. Webpack processes everything—JavaScript, Vue files, CSS, images—and transforms them into optimized assets that can run in the browser. This system worked well for years, and it's still widely used in existing projects.

However, Webpack-based build systems come with some tradeoffs. During development, your code must be bundled before it can run in the browser. Every time you save a file, Webpack needs to recompile part of your codebase, rebuild dependency graphs, and update the app in the browser. As projects grow, these rebuild times can become noticeable—sometimes several seconds, even for small changes.

That's where **Vite** offers a different approach.

Vite skips the bundling process entirely during development. Instead of compiling everything upfront, it uses the browser's native support for **ES modules** to load source files directly. When you run `npm run dev` in a Vite-powered app, it doesn't bundle your code. It serves your raw `.vue` and `.js` files as native modules. Only when you save a file does Vite recompile just that one file—and only if it changed. The result is near-instant updates, even in large codebases.

This distinction is key. Vue CLI uses Webpack to compile everything before serving it. Vite uses your source files directly, compiling only what's needed and only when it's needed.

If you're building a new Vue 3 project today, the official Vue documentation recommends using Vite unless you have a specific reason to stick with Vue CLI. For example, you might be maintaining a legacy Vue 2 application that already uses Vue CLI and Webpack. In that case, migrating everything to Vite may not be practical right away.

Let's take a closer look at how each tool creates a project.

Creating a project with Vue CLI:

```
npm install -g @vue/cli
vue create my-vue-cli-app
```

You'll get a prompt asking which features you want: Babel, TypeScript, Vue Router, Vuex, Linter, etc. It then installs a set of plugins and creates a Webpack-based project.

Once done, you can start the dev server with:

```
cd my-vue-cli-app
npm run serve
```

At this point, Vue CLI will bundle your project and start serving it at `localhost:8080`.

Now compare that with Vite:

```
npm create vite@latest
```

You'll be asked to name the project and pick a template (select `vue`). This creates a very lightweight scaffold with Vue 3 and the necessary tooling to get started.

Then:

```
cd my-vite-app
npm install
npm run dev
```

Vite starts the server in milliseconds. Any changes you make to `.vue` files, styles, or scripts are reflected in the browser instantly—without a full reload. This **Hot Module Replacement** (HMR) is faster and more consistent than what Vue CLI typically provides with Webpack.

Let's look at an example of how this affects your workflow.

Say you're editing a `ProductList.vue` component in a large Vue CLI project. You change one word in the template. Webpack must recompile the component, update the bundle, and send it to the browser. Depending on the size of the codebase, this can take a few seconds. That delay breaks your focus. In Vite, that same edit reflects in the browser instantly, because Vite compiled just the changed file and served it directly as a module.

Another practical difference comes in **build speed for production**. While Vite skips bundling during development, it **does bundle** for production— using Rollup, a fast and efficient module bundler that creates highly optimized, tree-shaken bundles.

38

This means:

During development, Vite is faster.

During production builds, Vite is still fast, but now benefits from Rollup's fine-grained optimizations.

Vue CLI relies on Webpack for both development and production, which can be slower in both stages—though still powerful and customizable.

What if you're used to the Vue CLI GUI?

Vue CLI comes with a graphical interface (`vue ui`) that lets you manage plugins, view project tasks, and run scripts in a more visual way. If you're a beginner or if your team prefers graphical tools, this can be helpful. Vite doesn't have a GUI. It expects you to use the terminal, scripts, and config files directly.

In practice, though, most teams using Vue at a professional level end up using terminal workflows, custom scripts, and CI/CD pipelines anyway—so the GUI is often less critical in the long run.

What about plugins and community support?

Vue CLI has a plugin-based architecture with plugins for Vue Router, Vuex, Babel, ESLint, and others. You can install these with a single command, and Vue CLI handles the configuration for you. Vite has a more manual approach: you install the packages and add the plugins yourself in `vite.config.js`. That might sound like a drawback, but in reality, it gives you more transparency and control.

For example, to add Vue Router in a Vite project, you run:

```
npm install vue-router
```

Then you configure it explicitly in your code, without relying on a generator to modify files for you. This encourages a deeper understanding of how the tooling works, which becomes valuable as your app grows or needs custom behavior.

If you are starting a new Vue 3 project today, and especially if you value speed, simplicity, and transparency in your build tools, **Vite is the clear choice**. It's faster during development, has less overhead, and is officially recommended for new projects.

If you are maintaining an existing Vue 2 application, or if you rely on specific Vue CLI plugins or Webpack customizations, then **Vue CLI still makes sense**. You don't need to migrate right away, and Vue CLI is still actively maintained.

However, for most use cases—especially for new development—Vite provides a faster, cleaner experience with better support for modern frontend workflows.

Debugging with Vue DevTools

As your Vue application becomes more complex, it becomes harder to mentally track what your components are doing, how reactive data is changing, and why certain parts of the UI may or may not be updating. This is exactly where **Vue DevTools** becomes invaluable.

Vue DevTools is a browser extension that lets you inspect the internal state and structure of your Vue application in real time. You can see the component hierarchy, check reactive data, observe prop values, trace events, monitor Vuex or Pinia state, and even time-travel through state mutations if you're using Vuex.

Installing Vue DevTools

Vue DevTools is available as a browser extension for both Chrome and Firefox.

For **Chrome**, go to the Chrome Web Store.

For **Firefox**, use the Add-ons site.

Once installed, open your Vue application in the browser. Then open your browser's developer tools (`F12` or `Ctrl+Shift+I`), and look for a new tab labeled **"Vue"**.

If your app is running in development mode, and Vue DevTools detects it properly, you'll see a live representation of your component tree.

If you don't see the Vue tab:

Make sure your app is running in development (`npm run dev`).

Make sure Vue is installed correctly.

Ensure your app is using Vue 3 (DevTools now works for both Vue 2 and 3, but support for 3 is better in newer versions).

Understanding the Component Tree

The first thing Vue DevTools shows you is your component tree. This is a live visual hierarchy of every component currently rendered in your application.

Let's say you have an `App.vue` that renders a `Header.vue`, a `ProductList.vue`, and a `Footer.vue`. Inside `ProductList.vue`, you might have several `ProductCard.vue` components—one for each product in a list.

In DevTools, you'll see this structure clearly:

```
App
├── Header
├── ProductList
│     ├── ProductCard
│     ├── ProductCard
│     └── ProductCard
└── Footer
```

Clicking on any of these components in the tree opens a side panel where you can inspect that component's **props**, **data**, **computed properties**, **emitted events**, and even **refs** declared inside its `setup()` function.

This is incredibly useful because you can now see your application's reactive state as it exists right now in the browser—not just what your code says, but what's actually happening live.

Inspecting Reactive Data

Let's use a concrete example. Suppose you have a counter component like this:

```
<template>
  <div>
    <p>Count: {{ count }}</p>
    <button @click="increment">+1</button>
  </div>
</template>

<script>
import { ref } from 'vue'

export default {
  name: 'Counter',
  setup() {
    const count = ref(0)

    const increment = () => {
      count.value++
    }

    return {
      count,
      increment
    }
  }
}
</script>
```

When you load this component in your app and open Vue DevTools, you'll see a `Counter` node in the component tree. Click it, and you'll see a section labeled **"Setup"** with a reactive `count` variable. You can even manually change its value directly in the DevTools panel and watch the UI update instantly.

This is one of the most helpful parts of debugging. You can test different values and state transitions without changing your source code or reloading the page. It's an interactive window into your app's reactivity system.

Debugging Props and Component Communication

Vue components often rely on props for communication. When something isn't behaving correctly—say, a component isn't showing the right data—Vue DevTools lets you inspect exactly what props were passed to that component.

Consider a simple `UserCard.vue`:

```
<template>
  <div>
    <h2>{{ name }}</h2>
    <p>Email: {{ email }}</p>
  </div>
</template>

<script setup>
defineProps({
  name: String,
  email: String
})
</script>
```

If the `UserCard` component appears blank or has missing data, you can open DevTools, select that instance, and immediately confirm whether `name` and `email` props were passed correctly. If not, you know the issue lies with the parent component, not the child.

This kind of visibility eliminates a lot of trial and error, especially in applications where many components are deeply nested or reused across different parts of the UI.

Tracking Events and Emissions

Another key feature is **event tracking**. If a component emits a custom event— for example, when a button is clicked—Vue DevTools logs that event in the panel.

Let's say you have a child component emitting an event like this:

```
<template>
  <button @click="$emit('increment')">+1</button>
</template>
```

In Vue DevTools, if you click this button in your app, you'll see an entry in the **Events** section showing:

Event emitted: increment

You can see which component emitted it and when, making it much easier to debug event-based communication between components.

Using DevTools with Vuex or Pinia

If you're using **Vuex** (Vue's traditional state management library) or **Pinia** (the new recommended store for Vue 3), Vue DevTools integrates directly with them. You can inspect the global store, watch state changes, and even replay past mutations or actions.

Let's use Vuex as an example.

In a Vuex-powered app, when your store changes—such as after calling a mutation or dispatching an action—DevTools logs it. You can click through these logs, inspect the state before and after, and track what changed.

This is especially powerful in complex apps where state flows through multiple components or asynchronous actions.

If you're using **Pinia**, DevTools automatically detects your stores and displays them in a dedicated section. You'll be able to see state values, getters, and actions, just like you would in Vuex—but with Pinia's simpler and more modern API.

Real-World Debugging Example

Suppose you're building an e-commerce dashboard. You have a `ProductList.vue` that fetches products from an API, a `ProductFilter.vue` to refine the list, and a `Cart.vue` that tracks added items.

Let's say filtering products doesn't work as expected. You click a filter, but the product list doesn't update.

Using Vue DevTools:

You open the `ProductFilter` component to confirm that the selected filter is changing as expected.

You check whether the `ProductList` component received the new props or reactive values.

You observe if a watcher or computed property that depends on the filter value is triggered.

If Vuex or Pinia is involved, you check if the store state changed after dispatching an action.

You confirm if the actual product list was re-fetched or re-computed based on the filter.

Without DevTools, each of these steps would require adding `console.log()` statements all over your code, refreshing the app repeatedly, and guessing where the bug might be. With DevTools, you pinpoint the problem in minutes.

Vue DevTools is not just a nice-to-have—it's essential when building anything beyond a small prototype. It gives you real-time access to your app's structure, reactive state, and internal behavior without needing to touch the source code. Whether you're debugging props, inspecting events, or tracing store mutations, DevTools allows you to understand what your app is really doing and why.

If you're serious about learning Vue, make DevTools part of your daily workflow. Keep it open while you develop. Check component state as you build. Use it not only when things break but also to confirm that things are working as expected.

Creating Your First Component

One of the most important concepts in Vue is the **component**. A component is a building block—a self-contained unit that encapsulates its own structure (HTML), behavior (JavaScript), and style (CSS). In Vue 3, every part of your interface, from buttons and cards to entire pages, is typically built as a component.

You've already seen the `App.vue` file that Vue creates for you by default. That's your **root component**, the one at the top of the application. Now you're going to create your **first custom component** that you can reuse and expand as your app grows.

We're going to build a very basic component called `Counter.vue`. This will be placed in the `src/components` folder. It will display a number, along with a button that increments the number every time it's clicked.

In your project, create a new file inside `src/components` called:

`Counter.vue`

Now open that file and write the following code:

```
<template>
  <div class="counter">
    <h2>Simple Counter</h2>
    <p>You clicked {{ count }} times.</p>
    <button @click="increment">Click Me</button>
  </div>
</template>

<script setup>
import { ref } from 'vue'

const count = ref(0)

const increment = () => {
  count.value++
}
</script>

<style scoped>
.counter {
  padding: 1rem;
  border: 1px solid #ddd;
  border-radius: 6px;
  max-width: 300px;
  font-family: sans-serif;
}
button {
  margin-top: 0.5rem;
  padding: 0.5rem 1rem;
  font-size: 1rem;
}
</style>
```

Let's pause here and explain what's happening, line by line.

Inside the `<template>`, we're defining the UI that will render in the browser. This includes:

A heading

A paragraph that shows the current count

A button that triggers the `increment()` function

Inside the `<script setup>` section, we're using Vue's Composition API. Specifically:

We import `ref()` from Vue, which creates a **reactive reference** to a value.

We initialize `count` with `ref(0)`, making it reactive so Vue can track changes to it.

We define an `increment()` function that simply adds 1 to the current count.

In the `<style scoped>` section, we add some basic styles to make the component look clean and readable. The `scoped` attribute ensures the styles apply only to this component, not globally across the app.

Using the Component in App.vue

Now that you've created your component, it's time to **register** and **render** it in the main application.

Open your `App.vue` file, which is in the `src` folder, and replace its content with the following:

```
<template>
  <div class="app">
    <h1>Vue 3 App with My First Component</h1>
    <Counter />
  </div>
</template>

<script setup>
import Counter from './components/Counter.vue'
</script>

<style>
.app {
```

```
    padding: 2rem;
    font-family: sans-serif;
}
</style>
```

Here's what's happening:

You import the `Counter` component using the `import` statement at the top of the `<script setup>`.

You use the `<Counter />` tag in the template to render the component.

Because we're using `<script setup>`, Vue automatically registers imported components—you don't need to manually register them with the `components` option.

Now save your files, return to your browser, and you'll see your component rendered on the page. When you click the button, the number updates instantly, thanks to Vue's reactivity system.

You've just written a **fully reactive, reusable component** using Vue 3's modern Composition API.

Why This Matters in Real Projects

You might be thinking: this is a very simple component. And that's true. But the principles here are exactly the same as what you'll use in much more complex applications.

Whether you're building a `TodoItem`, a `UserProfile`, or a `NotificationBanner`, every Vue component:

Encapsulates its own reactive state using `ref()` or `reactive()`

Provides interactivity with event listeners

Can be composed into larger layouts

Can communicate with other components using props and events

Starting with small, well-scoped components like this teaches you to break your application into manageable parts. This is one of the core reasons Vue apps scale well—you're always thinking in terms of components.

Exercise: Create a Reusable Alert Component

Let's do a small exercise to reinforce what you've just learned.

Your task: create a component called `Alert.vue` that accepts a `message` prop and displays it inside a styled alert box. If no message is provided, it should show a default message.

Create a new file in `src/components/Alert.vue` and try writing the following:

```
<template>
  <div class="alert">
    <p>{{ messageToShow }}</p>
  </div>
</template>

<script setup>
import { computed } from 'vue'

const props = defineProps({
  message: {
    type: String,
    default: 'This is a default alert message.'
  }
})

const messageToShow = computed(() => props.message)
</script>

<style scoped>
.alert {
  background-color: #ffe9e9;
  border: 1px solid #ff4d4d;
  padding: 1rem;
  border-radius: 5px;
  color: #b30000;
}
</style>
```

Now go back to `App.vue` and use it like this:

```
<template>
```

```
<div>
  <h1>Alert Component Example</h1>
  <Alert message="Something went wrong!" />
  <Alert />
</div>
</template>

<script setup>
import Alert from './components/Alert.vue'
</script>
```

This exercise teaches you how to:

Pass props into components

Use default prop values

Use computed properties to transform or expose reactive values

Encapsulate logic and styling in a clean, isolated way

These are the exact skills you'll use when building forms, dialogs, data displays, and dynamic UI elements.

You've now created your first Vue 3 component using the Composition API. You've defined reactive state using `ref()`, created interactive behavior, scoped styles to a component, and used that component inside your main application layout.

You've also seen how components can accept props and become reusable UI elements. These fundamentals are critical to every Vue project you'll ever build—whether you're designing a dashboard, a blog, a mobile interface, or a full e-commerce platform.

Chapter 3: The Essentials of Vue Templates and Reactivity

By now, you've seen how to create and use a basic Vue component. But to really understand Vue, you need to understand how its **template syntax** works, how it binds data to the DOM, how it responds to events, and how it updates the interface when the state changes.

This is where Vue's declarative design shines. Instead of manually updating the DOM when your data changes, Vue keeps your data and UI in sync automatically using its powerful **reactivity system**. You write the logic once, bind it to the template, and Vue handles the rest.

Template Syntax and Directives in Vue 3

One of the core ideas in Vue is that you describe what your UI should look like using **templates**. These templates are not just plain HTML—they are HTML enhanced with **Vue's declarative syntax**. This syntax allows you to bind your JavaScript state directly to your HTML, and it gives you special instructions—called **directives**—that control how the DOM behaves based on your data.

If you're coming from plain HTML and JavaScript, or even another framework like React, Vue's approach feels much more natural, especially for developers familiar with frontend markup. You can think of Vue templates as your HTML writing smartly "reacting" to your state.

How Vue Templates Work

In Vue, your component's `<template>` block is where you write markup. Inside it, you describe what the DOM should render based on your component's reactive state. You don't write `if` statements or loops in the usual JavaScript sense—instead, you use Vue's **template expressions** and **directives**.

Every expression you use inside the template is evaluated in the context of the component's setup state. For example, if you define a variable in your

`<script setup>` block using `ref()` or `reactive()`, you can reference it directly inside the template.

Here's a minimal example:

```
<template>
  <h1>Hello, {{ name }}</h1>
</template>

<script setup>
import { ref } from 'vue'

const name = ref('Ada')
</script>
```

In this example, `{{ name }}` is a **text interpolation** expression. Vue evaluates the `name` ref and displays its value in the DOM. If `name.value` changes later— let's say to `"Marie"`—the DOM will update automatically without you doing anything else.

This is the most basic form of template expression: **interpolation**.

Using Vue Directives

Now let's focus on directives. Vue provides special syntax for attributes in your HTML that starts with `v-`. These are called **directives**, and they tell Vue to apply some behavior to that element or binding.

Directives are what make your templates dynamic—they control how the element appears, how it behaves, and how it updates based on your data.

v-bind

You use `v-bind` when you want to bind an HTML attribute to a dynamic value. For instance, if you want to dynamically set the `src` of an image:

```
<template>
  <img v-bind:src="imageUrl" alt="Profile picture" />
</template>

<script setup>
import { ref } from 'vue'
```

```
const imageUrl =
ref('https://example.com/profile.jpg')
</script>
```

You can also use the shorthand : like this:

```
<img :src="imageUrl" alt="Profile picture" />
```

This works for **any HTML attribute**, including `href`, `class`, `id`, `disabled`, `placeholder`, and so on.

Here's a slightly more complex example using dynamic classes:

```
<template>
  <button :class="{ active: isActive }"
@click="toggleActive">
    Toggle Active
  </button>
</template>

<script setup>
import { ref } from 'vue'

const isActive = ref(false)

const toggleActive = () => {
  isActive.value = !isActive.value
}
</script>

<style scoped>
.active {
  background-color: green;
  color: white;
}
</style>
```

Here, the `:class` directive dynamically applies the `active` class when `isActive` is `true`. This kind of logic is common when building menus, tabs, or buttons that toggle state.

```
v-on
```

The `v-on` directive attaches event listeners. It's how you make your component respond to user input like clicks, keyboard presses, or form submissions.

Here's a basic example:

```
<template>
  <button v-on:click="increment">Increment</button>
</template>

<script setup>
import { ref } from 'vue'

const count = ref(0)

const increment = () => {
  count.value++
}
</script>
```

The shorthand for `v-on` is `@`, so this becomes:

```
<button @click="increment">Increment</button>
```
You can pass parameters too:

```
<button @click="greet('Sarah')">Greet</button>
```

And Vue supports **event modifiers**. Let's say you're working with a form:

```
<form @submit.prevent="handleSubmit">
  <input type="text" v-model="name" />
  <button type="submit">Submit</button>
</form>
```
The `.prevent` modifier stops the form's default submission behavior. Other modifiers include `.stop` (to stop event propagation), `.once` (only listen once), and `.capture`.

v-if, v-else-if, and v-else

Sometimes you want to conditionally show or hide elements based on the state. Vue makes this clean and readable with `v-if`.

```
<template>
```

```
  <p v-if="isLoggedIn">Welcome back!</p>
  <p v-else>Please log in.</p>
</template>

<script setup>
import { ref } from 'vue'

const isLoggedIn = ref(false)
</script>
```

Vue evaluates the condition and renders the correct block. If `isLoggedIn.value` becomes `true`, the first paragraph is shown. Otherwise, the `v-else` block is used.

If you need multiple conditions, use `v-else-if`:

```
<template>
  <p v-if="role === 'admin'">Admin panel</p>
  <p v-else-if="role === 'editor'">Editor tools</p>
  <p v-else>Viewer access only</p>
</template>

<script setup>
import { ref } from 'vue'

const role = ref('editor')
</script>
```

This reads exactly like a traditional `if/else if/else` block, but it's declarative and tied directly to your template.

`v-show`

There's a subtle but important difference between `v-if` and `v-show`. When you use `v-if`, Vue adds or removes the element from the DOM entirely. When you use `v-show`, Vue keeps the element in the DOM and toggles its `display` CSS property.

```
<p v-show="isVisible">This stays in the DOM, but
may be hidden.</p>
```

Use `v-if` when the condition is expensive to evaluate or the element is not needed at all unless the condition is true. Use `v-show` when toggling visibility frequently and you don't want Vue to remove/re-add the element.

v-for

This directive lets you render a list of items by looping over an array.

```
<template>
  <ul>
    <li v-for="item in items" :key="item.id">{{
item.name }}</li>
  </ul>
</template>

<script setup>
import { ref } from 'vue'

const items = ref([
  { id: 1, name: 'Banana' },
  { id: 2, name: 'Apple' },
  { id: 3, name: 'Cherry' }
])
</script>
```

Each `li` element gets rendered dynamically based on the array. The `:key` is critical—it tells Vue how to track changes to each item, which helps with performance and correctness during updates.

You can also get access to the index:

```
<li v-for="(item, index) in items" :key="item.id">
  {{ index }} - {{ item.name }}
</li>
```

This is useful for adding position markers or alternating styles.

Combining Directives

In practice, you'll often use several directives on the same element. For example:

```
<template>
```

```
  <button
    :class="{ active: isActive }"
    @click="toggle"
    v-if="visible"
  >
    Toggle Me
  </button>
</template>

<script setup>
import { ref } from 'vue'

const isActive = ref(false)
const visible = ref(true)

const toggle = () => {
  isActive.value = !isActive.value
}
</script>
```

This button is conditionally rendered, has dynamic styling, and reacts to a click—all with a few clear lines of code. This is the kind of declarative structure that makes Vue so productive and easy to maintain.

Practice Exercise: User Status Component

Let's reinforce what you've learned with a quick practical task.

Create a component that:

Displays a welcome message if a user is logged in

Shows a login button if not

Tracks whether the user is active or idle, and reflects this in the UI

```
<template>
  <div>
    <p v-if="loggedIn">Welcome, {{ username }}!</p>
    <button v-else @click="login">Log in</button>

    <p v-show="loggedIn">Status: {{ isActive ?
'Active' : 'Idle' }}</p>
```

```
     <button v-show="loggedIn"
@click="toggleStatus">Toggle Status</button>
   </div>
</template>

<script setup>
import { ref } from 'vue'

const loggedIn = ref(false)
const username = ref('Sam')
const isActive = ref(true)

const login = () => {
  loggedIn.value = true
}

const toggleStatus = () => {
  isActive.value = !isActive.value
}
</script>
```

Test it in your browser. You'll see how template expressions, `v-if`, `v-show`, `v-bind`, and event handling all come together to create a reactive, interactive component using clear and declarative syntax.

Vue's template syntax and directives are not just helpful—they're the core of how you build user interfaces in Vue. By understanding how interpolation, `v-bind`, `v-on`, `v-if`, `v-show`, and `v-for` work, you can describe almost any dynamic behavior in a clean, readable, and maintainable way.

The key thing to remember is that your template reflects your data. As the data changes, the DOM changes automatically. This is what makes Vue a reactive framework—and it all starts here with the syntax in your templates.

Data Binding and Interpolation in Vue 3

When you're building an interface with Vue, one of your primary tasks is connecting your application's **state**—your data—to the **user interface**. Vue gives you a concise and declarative way to do this, through a feature called **data binding**.

In plain terms, data binding means you write code that says, "this piece of data should appear here in the template," and Vue makes sure that what the user sees on the screen is always in sync with that data.

Text Interpolation with Double Curly Braces

Vue uses double curly braces (`{{ }}`) to bind text from your component logic into your template. This is one-way binding—from your data to the DOM.

Here's a simple example:

```
<template>
  <h1>Hello, {{ name }}</h1>
</template>

<script setup>
import { ref } from 'vue'

const name = ref('Ada')
</script>
```

When this component is rendered, it will show:

```
Hello, Ada
```

The value `name` is defined using Vue's Composition API via `ref()`, which creates a reactive reference to a string. Inside the template, you access it using `{{ name }}` without needing `.value`. Vue automatically unwraps refs inside templates for you.

Now, if the value of `name.value` changes—for example, in response to a user action—the template updates instantly.

Let's see that in action:

```
<template>
  <div>
    <h1>Hello, {{ name }}</h1>
    <button @click="name = 'Marie'">Change
Name</button>
  </div>
</template>
```

```
<script setup>
import { ref } from 'vue'

const name = ref('Ada')
</script>
```

When you click the button, the value of `name` changes, and Vue automatically re-renders the heading. You don't have to manually update the DOM. This is what makes Vue reactive—it tracks which parts of the template depend on which pieces of data and keeps everything synchronized for you.

HTML Attribute Binding with `v-bind`

Text content isn't the only thing you might want to bind dynamically. Often, you'll want to set or update an element's HTML **attributes**—like `src` for images, `href` for links, or `disabled` for form controls.

Vue provides the `v-bind` directive to make this possible.

Here's how it works:

```
<template>
  <img v-bind:src="imageUrl" alt="User photo" />
</template>

<script setup>
import { ref } from 'vue'

const imageUrl =
ref('https://example.com/photo.jpg')
</script>
```

Vue will evaluate the expression and assign it to the `src` attribute of the `img` tag. This means the image is loaded dynamically based on your data.

You can use the shorthand `:` instead of `v-bind:`:

```
<img :src="imageUrl" alt="User photo" />
```

This shorthand is more common and widely used in production code because it keeps your templates clean and readable.

Let's try another example—disabling a button based on a Boolean flag:

60

```
<template>
  <button :disabled="isSaving">Save</button>
</template>

<script setup>
import { ref } from 'vue'

const isSaving = ref(true)
</script>
```

When `isSaving` is `true`, the button will be disabled. If it becomes `false`, the button becomes clickable again. Vue updates the DOM automatically, with no manual intervention required.

Binding Class and Style

Vue also makes it easy to bind dynamic class names or styles. This is helpful when you want to apply visual cues based on the data—like changing the color of a message when it's an error.

Let's bind classes conditionally:

```
<template>
  <p :class="{ error: hasError }">Status
Message</p>
</template>

<script setup>
import { ref } from 'vue'

const hasError = ref(true)
</script>

<style scoped>
.error {
  color: red;
  font-weight: bold;
}
</style>
```

If `hasError` is `true`, the class `error` will be applied. If it's `false`, it won't. You can also combine multiple classes in an object or array syntax.

For inline styles:

```
<template>
  <p :style="{ fontSize: size + 'px' }">Resizable
Text</p>
</template>

<script setup>
import { ref } from 'vue'

const size = ref(24)
</script>
```

The style binding supports any valid CSS property name, and Vue will handle updating the element's inline styles when the data changes.

Two-Way Binding with `v-model`

Sometimes you don't just want to display data—you want to let the user **modify** it. This is where **two-way data binding** comes in.

Vue provides `v-model`, a directive that keeps a form input and a reactive variable in sync. When the input changes, the variable updates. When the variable updates, the input updates.

Let's build a working input field:

```
<template>
  <input v-model="name" placeholder="Enter your
name" />
  <p>Your name is: {{ name }}</p>
</template>

<script setup>
import { ref } from 'vue'

const name = ref('')
</script>
```

Here's what happens:

When the user types into the input, `name.value` changes.

When `name.value` changes (either through input or in code), the input reflects that change.

You can use `v-model` with all kinds of form elements: text inputs, checkboxes, radio buttons, selects, and even custom components.

A common real-world use case is handling form submissions. Here's a mini form example:

```
<template>
  <form @submit.prevent="submitForm">
    <label>
      Name:
      <input v-model="form.name" />
    </label>
    <label>
      Email:
      <input v-model="form.email" />
    </label>
    <button type="submit">Submit</button>
  </form>
</template>

<script setup>
import { reactive } from 'vue'

const form = reactive({
  name: '',
  email: ''
})

const submitForm = () => {
  console.log('Submitting:', form.name, form.email)
}
</script>
```

Notice how we're using `reactive()` instead of multiple `ref()`s to manage structured form data. This keeps the form state in one place and simplifies binding each field with `v-model`.

Data Binding in Real Applications

In a production application, you'll use data binding in many ways—especially for building responsive, dynamic interfaces. You might:

Bind image sources and alt text dynamically in a product gallery

Change button states based on validation or loading

Toggle styles for selected items in a list

Sync input fields to a search query and trigger filtered results

Dynamically update modal content or form fields based on selected data

Each of these relies on binding data from your component logic into your template and reacting to user interactions or asynchronous updates.

What makes Vue powerful is that all of this happens with minimal code. You declare how things should behave using bindings and expressions, and Vue manages the DOM updates automatically.

Practice Exercise: Profile Card with Bindings

To solidify what you've learned, build a `UserProfile.vue` component with the following behavior:

Display the user's name and photo

Bind the photo URL to an image tag

Add a checkbox to toggle admin status

Change the class of the name heading based on whether the user is an admin

Here's a working version:

```
<template>
  <div class="card">
    <img :src="user.photo" alt="User photo" />
    <h2 :class="{ admin: user.isAdmin }">{{
user.name }}</h2>

    <label>
      <input type="checkbox" v-model="user.isAdmin"
/>
      Admin
```

```
    </label>
  </div>
</template>

<script setup>
import { reactive } from 'vue'

const user = reactive({
  name: 'Ava Carter',
  photo: 'https://example.com/user.jpg',
  isAdmin: false
})
</script>

<style scoped>
.card {
  border: 1px solid #ccc;
  padding: 1rem;
  max-width: 300px;
}
.admin {
  color: red;
}
</style>
```

Try changing the `isAdmin` checkbox. The class on the heading will toggle in response. This is Vue's data binding system at work—efficient, declarative, and effortless once you understand the mechanics.

Data binding and interpolation are what make Vue reactive and expressive. You don't need to manually update the DOM or write glue code to keep your data in sync with the UI. Instead, you write what the UI should reflect, and Vue does the rest.

Handling Events and Methods in Vue 3

Once you've bound data to your interface using `ref()` or `reactive()`, the next step is to let users interact with that data—by clicking buttons, submitting forms, hovering over elements, and so on. Vue's event system is designed to make this clean, intuitive, and reactive.

You use the `v-on` directive to attach event listeners in your templates. This directive tells Vue, "when this event happens on this element, run this function."

Connecting a Button Click to a Method

Here's a basic example:

```
<template>
  <button @click="increment">Click Me</button>
  <p>You clicked {{ count }} times.</p>
</template>

<script setup>
import { ref } from 'vue'

const count = ref(0)

const increment = () => {
  count.value++
}
</script>
```

Here's what's happening:

We've defined a reactive value, `count`, which holds a number.

We've written a function, `increment()`, that adds one to the count.

We've used `@click="increment"` to connect the button's `click` event to the `increment` method.

Every time the user clicks the button, Vue calls the `increment` function, which changes the reactive data, and the DOM updates automatically.

The `@` is shorthand for `v-on`, so `@click` is equivalent to `v-on:click`. This shorthand is preferred because it keeps templates clean and readable.

Passing Arguments to Methods

Sometimes your method needs more information than just the event. For example, let's say you want to pass a number into your method to increase the count by a specific amount:

```
<template>
  <button @click="add(5)">Add 5</button>
  <p>Total: {{ total }}</p>
</template>

<script setup>
import { ref } from 'vue'

const total = ref(0)

const add = (amount) => {
  total.value += amount
}
</script>
```

When the user clicks the button, the add() function runs with the value 5 as its argument. The total variable updates accordingly, and the interface reflects the new value immediately.

If you also want to access the event object—for example, to prevent a default behavior—you can pass it as the second argument or use an inline function.

Here's how to access the click event directly:

```
<template>
  <button @click="handleClick($event)">Click with
Event</button>
</template>

<script setup>
const handleClick = (event) => {
  console.log('Clicked at:', event.clientX,
event.clientY)
}
</script>
```

This is useful when working with mouse coordinates, modifier keys, or custom event data.

Event Modifiers

Vue supports **modifiers** to make common event handling patterns easier and more readable.

Let's say you have a form that you want to handle entirely in JavaScript, without the browser submitting it by default. You can use the `.prevent` modifier:

```
<template>
  <form @submit.prevent="submitForm">
    <input type="text" v-model="name" />
    <button type="submit">Submit</button>
  </form>
</template>

<script setup>
import { ref } from 'vue'

const name = ref('')

const submitForm = () => {
  console.log('Form submitted with name:',
name.value)
}
</script>
```

The `.prevent` modifier on `@submit` calls `event.preventDefault()` automatically. You don't need to write that in your method—it's handled for you.

Vue offers other modifiers too:

`.stop` — calls `event.stopPropagation()`

`.once` — only listens to the event once

`.capture` — adds the event listener in capture mode

`.self` — only triggers the handler if the event was fired on the element itself

For example:

```
<button @click.stop="doSomething">Click without
bubbling</button>
```

This will prevent the click event from bubbling up to parent elements.

Using Keyboard Events

Vue also makes it simple to handle **keyboard input**, and you can use **keyboard event modifiers** to watch for specific keys.

For example:

```
<template>
  <input @keyup.enter="submitMessage" v-
model="message" />
</template>

<script setup>
import { ref } from 'vue'

const message = ref('')

const submitMessage = () => {
  console.log('Submitting message:', message.value)
}
</script>
```

Here, the `@keyup.enter` modifier listens specifically for the Enter key. You don't have to write extra logic to check which key was pressed—Vue handles that for you.

Other common key modifiers include:

`.esc`

`.tab`

`.delete`

`.arrow-up, .arrow-down, .arrow-left, .arrow-right`

This is incredibly useful for building forms, chat inputs, and search boxes.

Creating a Toggle Method

Let's go through a quick example that uses a method to toggle between two states:

```
<template>
  <button @click="toggle">Toggle
Visibility</button>
```

```
    <p v-if="visible">You can see me!</p>
</template>

<script setup>
import { ref } from 'vue'

const visible = ref(true)

const toggle = () => {
  visible.value = !visible.value
}
</script>
```

This is a classic example of a toggle function. You bind the button's click event to the `toggle()` method, which switches the Boolean `visible` between `true` and `false`. Vue handles the conditional rendering with `v-if`, and the paragraph appears or disappears accordingly.

This kind of interaction is common across all user interfaces—from showing or hiding modals and menus to toggling preferences and filters.

Methods Are Just Functions

It's worth saying explicitly: **methods in Vue 3's Composition API are just functions**. You don't need to put them in a `methods` block (as you did in Vue 2's Options API). You define them like any other function in JavaScript, inside the `<script setup>` block.

There's no special syntax or wrapper needed. This makes your code more flexible, easier to read, and more modular. You can even extract methods into reusable utilities (composables) when you want to reuse logic across components.

Exercise: Counter with Steps and Reset

Let's build a small component that combines everything we've discussed—reactive state, event binding, method calls, and modifiers.

```
<template>
  <h2>Counter: {{ count }}</h2>

  <button @click="increment(1)">+1</button>
  <button @click="increment(5)">+5</button>
```

```
  <button @click="reset">Reset</button>

  <form @submit.prevent="submitCount">
    <input v-model.number="count" type="number" />
    <button type="submit">Submit Count</button>
  </form>
</template>

<script setup>
import { ref } from 'vue'

const count = ref(0)

const increment = (amount) => {
  count.value += amount
}

const reset = () => {
  count.value = 0
}

const submitCount = () => {
  alert(`Count submitted: ${count.value}`)
}
</script>
```

Here's what's happening:

We bind the count to display and control elements.

The `increment` method adjusts the count by a given amount.

The `reset` method sets it back to zero.

The form lets users type in a number and submit it, with `.prevent` stopping the page reload.

This is a real, working pattern used in dashboards, settings panels, games, forms, and more.

Event handling in Vue is direct, flexible, and tightly integrated with the reactivity system. You write standard JavaScript functions and connect them to your templates using the `v-on` directive—or more commonly, its shorthand `@`.

Whether you're responding to clicks, capturing keyboard input, submitting forms, or toggling visibility, Vue provides a clean and consistent way to handle interaction without boilerplate.

What makes this especially powerful is that Vue automatically watches for reactive data changes inside those methods and updates the UI in sync. You never have to tell Vue to re-render anything.

Conditional Rendering and Loops

When you build user interfaces, you almost always need to make decisions about what should appear on the screen. Should a button be shown or hidden? Should a message be displayed when a list is empty? Should certain content only be visible for logged-in users?

These kinds of conditions are handled through **conditional rendering**. In Vue, you can use directives like `v-if`, `v-else-if`, `v-else`, and `v-show` to control whether an element appears in the DOM.

Alongside that, Vue also gives you a way to render items **repeatedly**—for example, looping through an array of products and displaying a card for each one. This is handled with `v-for`.

Conditional Rendering with `v-if`

The most direct way to control whether an element is included in the DOM is with the `v-if` directive. Vue evaluates the expression passed to `v-if`, and if it's `true`, the element is rendered. If it's `false`, the element is removed from the DOM completely.

Here's a basic example:

```
<template>
  <p v-if="isLoggedIn">Welcome back, user!</p>
  <p v-else>Please log in to continue.</p>
</template>
```

```
<script setup>
import { ref } from 'vue'

const isLoggedIn = ref(false)
</script>
```

When `isLoggedIn` is `false`, the second paragraph is shown. When it becomes `true`, the first one appears and the second disappears.

You can also chain multiple conditions using `v-else-if`:

```
<template>
  <p v-if="status === 'loading'">Loading...</p>
  <p v-else-if="status === 'success'">Data loaded
successfully.</p>
  <p v-else-if="status === 'error'">Something went
wrong.</p>
  <p v-else>Status unknown.</p>
</template>

<script setup>
import { ref } from 'vue'

const status = ref('loading') // try changing this
to 'success' or 'error'
</script>
```

Vue evaluates each condition in order and renders the first one that returns `true`.

This setup is commonly used when handling network requests, authentication states, or switching between different views of the same component.

Toggling Visibility with `v-show`

While `v-if` adds or removes elements from the DOM, the `v-show` directive works differently. The element is always in the DOM, but Vue uses inline CSS (`display: none`) to hide or show it.

```
<template>
  <p v-show="isVisible">This is always in the DOM
but may be hidden.</p>
</template>
```

```
<script setup>
import { ref } from 'vue'

const isVisible = ref(true)
</script>
```

So, which one should you use?

Use `v-if` when:

The condition rarely changes

You want the element removed entirely when not needed

You're dealing with large sections of the DOM or expensive components

Use `v-show` when:

You toggle visibility frequently (like dropdowns, tabs, or tooltips)

The cost of keeping the element in the DOM is low

They serve different needs, and understanding the trade-offs helps you make good performance decisions.

Rendering Lists with `v-for`

Now let's shift to loops.

Vue's `v-for` directive lets you render an element or component for every item in a collection—usually an array. This is especially common when displaying a list of items like blog posts, products, or users.

Here's a basic example:

```
<template>
  <ul>
    <li v-for="fruit in fruits" :key="fruit">{{
fruit }}</li>
  </ul>
</template>

<script setup>
import { ref } from 'vue'
```

```
const fruits = ref(['Apple', 'Banana', 'Cherry'])
</script>
```

Vue repeats the `<li>` for each fruit in the array. The `:key` attribute is required and must be unique—it helps Vue track which items changed, so it can update the DOM efficiently.

If you're looping over an array of objects, you can use a property as the key:

```
<template>
  <ul>
    <li v-for="user in users" :key="user.id">
      {{ user.name }} - {{ user.email }}
    </li>
  </ul>
</template>

<script setup>
import { ref } from 'vue'

const users = ref([
  { id: 1, name: 'Sarah', email:
'sarah@example.com' },
  { id: 2, name: 'Daniel', email:
'daniel@example.com' },
  { id: 3, name: 'Amina', email:
'amina@example.com' }
])
</script>
```

You can also access the current index if needed:

```
<li v-for="(user, index) in users" :key="user.id">
  {{ index + 1 }}. {{ user.name }}
</li>
```

That's useful for numbering rows in a table or alternating styles.

Combining v-if and v-for

You might sometimes want to conditionally render content **inside** a loop. That's perfectly fine, but you should **not** put v-if and v-for on the same element if you can avoid it. Vue processes `v-for` before `v-if`, which can lead to unexpected behavior.

Instead, use computed properties or filter the array beforehand, like this:

```
<template>
  <ul>
    <li v-for="task in completedTasks"
:key="task.id">
      {{ task.title }}
    </li>
  </ul>
</template>

<script setup>
import { ref, computed } from 'vue'

const tasks = ref([
  { id: 1, title: 'Buy milk', done: true },
  { id: 2, title: 'Write email', done: false },
  { id: 3, title: 'Read article', done: true }
])

const completedTasks = computed(() => {
  return tasks.value.filter(task => task.done)
})
</script>
```

This keeps your templates clean and avoids performance pitfalls. Instead of checking `v-if="task.done"` inside the loop, you filter the list before it reaches the DOM.

Example: Product List with Stock Status

Let's apply both conditional rendering and looping in a practical example. Suppose you're building a product catalog and want to:

Show a list of products

Indicate whether each product is in stock

Display a message when no products are available

Here's how you might write that:

```
<template>
  <div>
    <h2>Product List</h2>

    <p v-if="products.length === 0">No products
available.</p>

    <ul v-else>
      <li v-for="product in products"
:key="product.id">
        {{ product.name }} -
        <span v-if="product.inStock">In
Stock</span>
        <span v-else>Out of Stock</span>
      </li>
    </ul>
  </div>
</template>

<script setup>
import { ref } from 'vue'

const products = ref([
  { id: 1, name: 'Phone', inStock: true },
  { id: 2, name: 'Laptop', inStock: false },
  { id: 3, name: 'Headphones', inStock: true }
])
</script>
```

This approach shows all the building blocks in action:

v-if to conditionally show a fallback message

v-else to render the list only when it's not empty

v-for to loop through the list

v-if inside the loop to display different labels based on stock status

This is a pattern you'll see in real-world dashboards, e-commerce sites, and admin panels.

Exercise: To-Do List with Status Filter

Let's write a small to-do list that:

Shows all tasks

Displays only the ones marked as "completed" if a filter is active

Displays a message when the filtered list is empty

```
<template>
  <h2>My Tasks</h2>

  <label>
    <input type="checkbox" v-
model="showCompletedOnly" />
    Show completed only
  </label>

  <p v-if="filteredTasks.length === 0">No tasks to
show.</p>

  <ul v-else>
    <li v-for="task in filteredTasks"
:key="task.id">
      {{ task.title }} <span v-
if="task.done">(Done)</span>
    </li>
  </ul>
</template>

<script setup>
import { ref, computed } from 'vue'

const showCompletedOnly = ref(false)

const tasks = ref([
  { id: 1, title: 'Finish report', done: true },
  { id: 2, title: 'Clean inbox', done: false },
  { id: 3, title: 'Book meeting', done: false }
])

const filteredTasks = computed(() => {
  if (showCompletedOnly.value) {
    return tasks.value.filter(task => task.done)
```

```
    } else {
      return tasks.value
    }
})
</script>
```

This exercise brings everything together—state, conditionals, loops, filtering, and reactivity. As you change the checkbox, Vue automatically recalculates the filtered list and updates the DOM.

Conditional rendering and loops are at the core of how you create interactive, data-driven interfaces in Vue. They give you precise control over what appears in the DOM and how content changes based on user input or reactive state.

By understanding how `v-if`, `v-show`, `v-for`, and computed properties work together, you're able to build flexible and maintainable UIs—ones that scale smoothly from small widgets to full-featured applications.

Understanding `ref()` and `reactive()` in Vue 3

Vue's reactivity system is what allows your data to drive your interface. You declare a piece of state, bind it to your template, and Vue handles keeping the DOM in sync when the state changes. That works because Vue tracks reactive values and knows when to update the UI.

In Vue 3's Composition API, there are two primary ways to declare reactive data: `ref()` and `reactive()`.

`ref()`: Creating Reactive Primitive Values

When you want to create a reactive value—like a string, number, boolean, or even a single object reference—you use `ref()`.

Here's the most basic use case:

```
<script setup>
import { ref } from 'vue'

const counter = ref(0)
```

```
</script>

<template>
  <p>Counter: {{ counter }}</p>
  <button @click="counter++">Increment</button>
</template>
```

When you use `ref(0)`, Vue wraps the number 0 inside a **reactive reference object**. This object has a `.value` property that holds the actual value.

Inside JavaScript code, you access or update it using `counter.value`. But inside the template, Vue automatically unwraps it, so you can use `{{ counter }}` without the `.value`.

Let's look at this from the JavaScript perspective:

```
counter.value++            // this changes the value
console.log(counter.value)  // logs the current
value
```

This `.value` pattern is consistent for all refs, regardless of whether the value is a primitive, an object, or an array. In fact, you can put anything inside a ref:

```
const name = ref('Sarah')
const isActive = ref(true)
const age = ref(25)
const products = ref(['phone', 'laptop',
'headphones'])
```

Even though you can use arrays or objects inside `ref()`, there's a key difference in how Vue handles reactivity depending on the structure. That's where `reactive()` becomes useful.

`reactive()`: Creating Reactive Objects

When you're dealing with an object that has multiple properties—especially if those properties are going to be accessed or updated independently—it's often better to use `reactive()`.

```
<script setup>
import { reactive } from 'vue'

const user = reactive({
```

```
  name: 'Sarah',
  email: 'sarah@example.com',
  age: 30
})
</script>

<template>
  <h2>User Profile</h2>
  <p>Name: {{ user.name }}</p>
  <p>Email: {{ user.email }}</p>
  <p>Age: {{ user.age }}</p>
</template>
```

When you use `reactive()`, Vue converts the object into a **deeply reactive proxy**. Every property inside the object is tracked automatically. That means any change to `user.name` or `user.age` will trigger updates to the DOM where those values are used.

And unlike `ref()`, with `reactive()` you **don't use** `.value`. You just access properties directly:

```
user.name = 'Daniel'        // this updates the
reactive property
console.log(user.age)       // logs current age
```

This syntax is more natural when working with structured data, like form models, configuration objects, or component settings.

Differences in Behavior

Here's the key conceptual difference:

`ref()` is a wrapper around a single value.

`reactive()` creates a proxy that makes an entire object reactive.

They both return reactive data, and they both work with Vue's rendering system. But their usage and ergonomics are different.

If you wrap an object inside `ref()`:

```
const settings = ref({ darkMode: true, layout:
'grid' })
```

You now have to access nested properties like this:

```
settings.value.darkMode = false
```

That `.value` access becomes awkward when you need to reference properties often. In this case, using `reactive()` would simplify your code:

```
const settings = reactive({ darkMode: true, layout: 'grid' })

settings.darkMode = false
```

On the other hand, `ref()` shines when you need:

A single value (e.g., a number, string, boolean)

To track an element or DOM reference (`ref(null)`)

To preserve reactivity in a variable that will be reassigned entirely

A Real Example: Form State

Say you're building a form where a user can enter their name and email. Here's how you could manage that state with `ref()` and `reactive()`.

Using `ref()` for each field:

```
<script setup>
import { ref } from 'vue'

const name = ref('')
const email = ref('')

const submitForm = () => {
  console.log('Submitting:', name.value,
email.value)
}
</script>

<template>
  <form @submit.prevent="submitForm">
    <input v-model="name" placeholder="Name" />
    <input v-model="email" placeholder="Email" />
    <button type="submit">Submit</button>
```

```
    </form>
</template>
```

This works well, especially for simple forms. But if you have many fields, managing each one with its own ref becomes repetitive.

Here's the same form using `reactive()`:

```
<script setup>
import { reactive } from 'vue'

const form = reactive({
  name: '',
  email: ''
})

const submitForm = () => {
  console.log('Submitting:', form.name, form.email)
}
</script>

<template>
  <form @submit.prevent="submitForm">
    <input v-model="form.name" placeholder="Name"
/>
    <input v-model="form.email" placeholder="Email"
/>
    <button type="submit">Submit</button>
  </form>
</template>
```

Now your form fields are managed in a single reactive object. You can pass the whole object around, validate it, reset it, or serialize it as needed. This is often cleaner and more scalable.

Can You Use Them Together?

Yes—and you often will.

You might use `reactive()` for your main state object, and `ref()` for individual flags or counters:

```
const form = reactive({
```

```
  name: '',
  email: ''
})

const submitting = ref(false)

const submitForm = async () => {
  submitting.value = true
  await sendToServer(form)
  submitting.value = false
}
```

This lets you model state in the way that makes the most sense for each piece of data.

Watching Refs and Reactives

Both `ref()` and `reactive()` are compatible with Vue's reactivity utilities like `watch()` and `computed()`.

For example, to watch a `ref()`:

```
watch(name, (newVal, oldVal) => {
  console.log(`Name changed from ${oldVal} to
${newVal}`)
})
```

To watch a property inside a reactive object:

```
watch(() => form.email, (newVal) => {
  console.log('Email changed:', newVal)
})
```

This syntax gives you full control over tracking changes and triggering side effects—like form validation, saving to storage, or calling APIs.

Exercise: Login Form with Validation

Let's practice what you've learned.

Create a component with:

A form using `reactive()` for state

A `ref()` for error messages

A submit button that simulates validation

```
<script setup>
import { reactive, ref } from 'vue'

const form = reactive({
  username: '',
  password: ''
})

const errorMessage = ref('')

const submit = () => {
  if (!form.username || !form.password) {
    errorMessage.value = 'All fields are required.'
    return
  }

  errorMessage.value = ''
  alert(`Logging in as ${form.username}`)
}
</script>

<template>
  <form @submit.prevent="submit">
    <input v-model="form.username"
placeholder="Username" />
    <input v-model="form.password" type="password"
placeholder="Password" />
    <p v-if="errorMessage">{{ errorMessage }}</p>
    <button type="submit">Login</button>
  </form>
</template>
```

This example uses both `ref()` and `reactive()` in the same component, reflecting how real apps manage different kinds of state.

Vue's Composition API gives you low-level access to the reactivity system, and `ref()` and `reactive()` are the main tools for making data reactive. Once you understand how they work, you can confidently manage state in any component, feature, or module.

85

Chapter 4: Components and Communication

As your Vue application grows, one of the most important skills you'll need is knowing how to **break your interface into components** and make them talk to each other in a clean, maintainable way.

In earlier chapters, you created standalone components like `Counter.vue` or `UserCard.vue`. Now, you're going to learn how to reuse those components, how to pass information down to them using **props**, how to receive events back up from them using **custom events**, and how to organize your components so they don't become a tangled mess.

Creating Reusable Components

Reusability is a core principle of modern frontend development. Instead of duplicating markup and logic across different parts of your application, you should extract that repeated functionality into a well-designed, self-contained component.

A reusable component in Vue is one that:

Accepts **props** to make it flexible

Emits **events** to report changes or interactions

Encapsulates its own logic and styling

Can be used in multiple places without modification

When you build with reusability in mind, you reduce maintenance, improve readability, and make your components easier to test and extend.

A Practical Example: BaseButton Component

You'll often have several types of buttons in your UI—some primary, some secondary, some disabled, some with icons. Instead of writing `<button>` tags in multiple components and repeating logic or styling, you can build a

BaseButton.vue that handles the common behavior and appearance, but still allows customization.

Create a file in src/components/base/BaseButton.vue:

```
<template>
  <button
    :class="['base-button', variantClass, {
disabled }]"
    :disabled="disabled"
    @click="handleClick"
  >
    <slot>Click</slot>
  </button>
</template>

<script setup>
import { computed } from 'vue'

const props = defineProps({
  variant: {
    type: String,
    default: 'primary', // can be 'primary',
'secondary', etc.
  },
  disabled: {
    type: Boolean,
    default: false,
  },
})

const emit = defineEmits(['click'])

const handleClick = (event) => {
  if (!props.disabled) {
    emit('click', event)
  }
}

const variantClass = computed(() => {
  return `variant-${props.variant}`
})
</script>
```

```
<style scoped>
.base-button {
  padding: 0.6rem 1.2rem;
  border: none;
  border-radius: 4px;
  font-size: 1rem;
  cursor: pointer;
  transition: background-color 0.2s ease;
}

.variant-primary {
  background-color: #2a7dfd;
  color: white;
}

.variant-secondary {
  background-color: #f0f0f0;
  color: #333;
}

.disabled {
  background-color: #cccccc;
  color: #888;
  cursor: not-allowed;
}
</style>
```

Let's walk through what this component does:

It accepts a `variant` prop that controls styling.

It accepts a `disabled` prop to control both appearance and behavior.

It emits a `click` event **only if** the button is not disabled.

It renders whatever content is passed in via a `<slot>`—so it's not tied to any specific label or icon.

This makes the component highly reusable. It can be used across your app in many forms:

```
<BaseButton @click="saveData">Save</BaseButton>
```

```
<BaseButton variant="secondary"
@click="cancelForm">Cancel</BaseButton>
<BaseButton
:disabled="isLoading">Submit</BaseButton>
```

If you need to show a loading spinner, change colors, or wrap the content in an icon, you can extend this base component without rewriting its internals.

Component Design Guidelines

When designing reusable components, a few principles can help you stay consistent and scalable.

Keep your component focused.
A reusable component should do one thing and do it well. A `BaseButton` handles interaction and appearance. It should not handle API calls, manage application state, or make assumptions about its context.

Expose flexibility through props.
Allow the parent component to control the behavior. For example, you don't hardcode text or colors—you accept them as props, or expose slots for full customization.

Emit events instead of triggering logic directly.
Reusable components should not directly perform side effects. Instead, they emit events and let the parent decide what to do in response. This decouples the component from the rest of the system.

Avoid internal dependencies.
Don't tightly couple your reusable components to app-specific stores, routes, or external APIs. That makes them harder to reuse. Let the parent pass what the component needs.

Extending Reusability: Component Composition

Sometimes, instead of a single standalone component, you'll create a set of small components that work together.

For example, say you have a `BaseInput.vue`:

```
<template>
  <div class="input-group">
```

```
    <label v-if="label">{{ label }}</label>
    <input
      :type="type"
      :value="modelValue"
      @input="$emit('update:modelValue',
$event.target.value)"
      :placeholder="placeholder"
    />
  </div>
</template>

<script setup>
defineProps({
  modelValue: String,
  label: String,
  type: {
    type: String,
    default: 'text'
  },
  placeholder: String
})

defineEmits(['update:modelValue'])
</script>
```

This input uses the `v-model` binding convention, where the parent component can bind to `modelValue` and receive updates.

Now you can use it in any form like this:

```
<BaseInput v-model="email" label="Email"
placeholder="you@example.com" />
```

You've now created an input field that supports labels, placeholders, and two-way binding—and you didn't have to duplicate logic. If the project needs inputs with validation, icons, or helper text, you can keep extending `BaseInput.vue` or compose it into larger form components.

Exercise: Build a Reusable Card Component

Let's build another practical reusable component: `BaseCard.vue`. This will be a visual container that can accept dynamic content.

```
<template>
```

```
<div class="card">
  <header v-if="$slots.header" class="card-header">
    <slot name="header" />
  </header>

  <main class="card-body">
    <slot />
  </main>

  <footer v-if="$slots.footer" class="card-footer">
    <slot name="footer" />
  </footer>
</div>
</template>

<style scoped>
.card {
  border: 1px solid #ddd;
  border-radius: 8px;
  background: white;
  padding: 1rem;
  max-width: 400px;
}

.card-header,
.card-footer {
  margin-bottom: 1rem;
}

.card-footer {
  margin-top: 1rem;
}
</style>
```

Now use it like this:

```
<BaseCard>
  <template #header>
    <h3>Product Info</h3>
  </template>
```

```
  <p>This is a simple reusable card component.</p>

  <template #footer>
    <button @click="showMore">View Details</button>
  </template>
</BaseCard>
```

This kind of pattern is perfect for layout and UI structure components. You give the base component responsibility for the layout, and the parent decides what content to put inside.

Managing Reusable Component Folders

As your component library grows, you'll want to keep reusable UI components separated from application-specific ones. A good structure looks like this:

`src/`

`├── components/`

`|     ├── base/`   ← base UI primitives

`|     ├── layout/`   ← layout elements like AppShell, Header, Sidebar`

`|     ├── forms/`   ← composed form inputs and wrappers

`|     ├── features/`   ← domain-specific components like UserProfile.vue`

In this structure:

`base/` holds truly generic components like `BaseButton.vue`, `BaseInput.vue`, `BaseCard.vue`.

`layout/` holds structural UI pieces that wrap whole pages.

`features/` includes business-specific components that may not be reused across domains.

This separation keeps things organized and makes it easier to refactor, test, and extend your components in the future.

Creating reusable components in Vue 3 is not just about writing smaller `.vue` files. It's about thinking in terms of **interfaces**, **encapsulation**, and **communication boundaries**. A well-designed reusable component:

Accepts the inputs it needs (via props)

Sends out the events it generates (via emits)

Lets you control the presentation (via slots or styling)

Does not assume where or how it's used

This makes your components portable, testable, and easier to integrate into new features or even new projects.

Props and Custom Events

Vue components are designed to be **modular and self-contained**, but they rarely operate in complete isolation. Components need to **receive data** from a parent and often need to **communicate back** when something happens.

This is where props and custom events come in:

Props allow the parent to pass data *down* to a child.

Custom events allow the child to send information *up* to the parent.

These are the two essential tools for communication between components. Vue intentionally keeps this model simple and unidirectional, making it easy to reason about how data flows through your application.

Using Props to Pass Data from Parent to Child

In Vue, a **prop** is a value that the parent component provides to the child. Props are declared in the child component using `defineProps()` and passed in from the parent as attributes.

Here's a basic example:

```
<!-- ProductCard.vue -->
<template>
  <div class="product-card">
```

```
    <h3>{{ title }}</h3>
    <p>${{ price.toFixed(2) }}</p>
  </div>
</template>

<script setup>
defineProps({
  title: String,
  price: Number
})
</script>
```

Now the parent component can use `ProductCard.vue` like this:

```
<ProductCard title="Laptop" :price="999.99" />
```

The child component is now receiving two pieces of data—`title` and `price`—that it can render or use for logic.

You can also use default values and type validation:

```
defineProps({
  title: {
    type: String,
    default: 'Untitled Product'
  },
  price: {
    type: Number,
    required: true
  }
})
```

This ensures that your component remains predictable, even when some props are missing or passed incorrectly.

Let's now look at a more dynamic example—passing an object.

```
<!-- UserProfile.vue -->
<template>
  <div>
    <h2>{{ user.name }}</h2>
    <p>Email: {{ user.email }}</p>
  </div>
</template>
```

```
<script setup>
defineProps({
  user: Object
})
</script>
```

Used like this in a parent:

```
<UserProfile :user="{ name: 'Amina', email:
'amina@example.com' }" />
```

The component stays simple and flexible, and the parent has full control over the data being passed in.

Vue's reactivity system ensures that if the parent updates the prop value, the child will reflect the change automatically.

Emitting Events from Child to Parent

While props are used for data going **into** a component, **custom events** are used to send signals **out of** the component. The most common use case is when a child component detects an action—like a click or form submission—and needs to notify the parent.

Let's enhance our `ProductCard.vue` to emit an event when the user clicks an "Add to Cart" button.

```
<!-- ProductCard.vue -->
<template>
  <div class="product-card">
    <h3>{{ title }}</h3>
    <p>${{ price.toFixed(2) }}</p>
    <button @click="addToCart">Add to Cart</button>
  </div>
</template>

<script setup>
const props = defineProps({
  title: String,
  price: Number
})
```

```
const emit = defineEmits(['add-to-cart'])

const addToCart = () => {
  emit('add-to-cart', {
    name: props.title,
    price: props.price
  })
}
</script>
```

Then, in the parent component:

```
<ProductCard
  title="Laptop"
  :price="999.99"
  @add-to-cart="handleAdd"
/>

<script setup>
const handleAdd = (product) => {
  console.log('Product added:', product)
}
</script>
```

Here's what's happening:

The child emits an event named 'add-to-cart' using emit('add-to-cart', data)

The parent listens for that event using @add-to-cart

When the event fires, the parent executes handleAdd and receives the payload

This keeps your component decoupled. The child doesn't need to know what happens when the button is clicked—it simply emits an event. The parent decides what to do with it.

Event Naming and Best Practices

Event names in Vue are typically kebab-case (add-to-cart, save-profile, update-status) and descriptive of what just happened. Avoid names like clicked or changed that are vague or conflict with native events.

You can emit any kind of data with the event—a string, number, object, or even nothing. You can also emit multiple different event types from the same component.

For example:

```
defineEmits(['submit', 'cancel', 'delete'])
```

And each can carry different types of payloads depending on context.

Keep in mind that **custom events do not bubble** up the DOM. They go only to the **direct parent** component. If you need to emit data multiple levels upward, consider using an intermediate wrapper component or state management (like Pinia or Vuex).

Two-Way Binding with `v-model`

In many cases, you want a child component to expose a value that can be bound using `v-model`. Vue 3 lets you create custom two-way bindings using `modelValue` as the prop and `update:modelValue` as the event.

Here's an example with a custom input component:

```
<!-- BaseInput.vue -->
<template>
  <input :value="modelValue"
@input="$emit('update:modelValue',
$event.target.value)" />
</template>

<script setup>
defineProps(['modelValue'])
defineEmits(['update:modelValue'])
</script>
```

Now you can use this component like this:

```
<BaseInput v-model="username" />
```

And in your script:

```
const username = ref('')
```

Any change in the input updates `username`, and any change to `username` updates the input. This is extremely useful for building custom form inputs, checkboxes, dropdowns, sliders, and even complex inputs like date pickers.

Practical Exercise: Reusable Rating Component

Let's build a component that:

Accepts a `rating` prop

Renders 1–5 stars

Emits a new rating when the user clicks a star

```html
<!-- RatingStars.vue -->
<template>
  <div>
    <span
      v-for="star in 5"
      :key="star"
      :class="{ selected: star <= rating }"
      @click="$emit('update:rating', star)"
    >
      ★
    </span>
  </div>
</template>

<script setup>
defineProps({
  rating: Number
})

defineEmits(['update:rating'])
</script>

<style scoped>
.selected {
  color: gold;
}
span {
  font-size: 1.5rem;
  cursor: pointer;
```

```
}
</style>
```

Use it like this:

```
<RatingStars v-model:rating="productRating" />

<script setup>
const productRating = ref(3)
</script>
```

Now you've created a fully interactive and reusable star-rating component, using props to accept initial state, events to report changes, and `v-model` to make it seamless to bind.

Props and custom events are the foundation of communication in Vue. They enforce a clear, predictable structure:

Data flows **down** from parent to child using **props**

Events bubble **up** from child to parent using **custom events**

This one-way data flow makes your components easier to test, debug, and reuse. It encourages loose coupling and modular design, which is key for building scalable applications.

Understanding Slots in Vue 3

By default, when you define a Vue component, you control its structure and template. But what if you want to create a component like a card or a modal that should render different content depending on how and where it's used?

Hardcoding the content inside the component makes it rigid. That's where **slots** come in.

A slot is a placeholder for content provided by the component's parent. When a component defines a `<slot>`, it is saying: *"I will render whatever content the parent gives me, right here."*

Creating a Flexible Layout with Default Slots

Suppose you want to build a reusable `BaseCard.vue` component that wraps content in a styled box.

```
<!-- BaseCard.vue -->
<template>
  <div class="card">
    <slot />
  </div>
</template>

<style scoped>
.card {
  border: 1px solid #ddd;
  border-radius: 8px;
  background: #fff;
  padding: 1.5rem;
  box-shadow: 0 2px 4px rgba(0,0,0,0.1);
}
</style>
```

Here, `<slot />` is a placeholder. The card doesn't care what content gets inserted—it just knows *where* to render it.

Now use it in a parent component:

```
<BaseCard>
  <h2>Welcome</h2>
  <p>This is a custom message inside the card.</p>
</BaseCard>
```

When this renders, the content inside `<BaseCard>` gets inserted at the slot location. The card provides structure and styling; the parent provides content. This keeps both components clean and maintainable.

Named Slots for Custom Sections

There are many cases where you want to allow the parent to provide content for multiple specific areas. For example, you might want a card with a header, body, and footer—all customizable.

Vue allows this using **named slots**. Each slot gets a name, and the parent provides content for each one using `<template #slotName>`.

Let's extend `BaseCard.vue`:

```
<template>
  <div class="card">
    <header v-if="$slots.header" class="card-header">
      <slot name="header" />
    </header>

    <main class="card-body">
      <slot />
    </main>

    <footer v-if="$slots.footer" class="card-footer">
      <slot name="footer" />
    </footer>
  </div>
</template>

<style scoped>
.card {
  border: 1px solid #ccc;
  border-radius: 8px;
  padding: 1rem;
  background-color: white;
}
.card-header {
  font-weight: bold;
  margin-bottom: 1rem;
}
.card-footer {
  margin-top: 1rem;
  font-size: 0.9rem;
  color: #666;
}
</style>
```

And now in the parent:

```
<BaseCard>
  <template #header>
    <h3>User Details</h3>
  </template>
```

```
  <p>Name: Amina Carter</p>
  <p>Email: amina@example.com</p>

  <template #footer>
    Last updated: 2 hours ago
  </template>
</BaseCard>
```

Each part of the layout can now be customized by the parent. The card itself remains completely reusable, and the logic is clearly separated between structure and content.

Vue automatically detects whether content was provided for a named slot using `$slots.slotName`, allowing you to optionally render headers or footers only when needed.

Scoped Slots for Data Sharing

Sometimes, the child component needs to expose data to the parent *within the slot*. This is handled with **scoped slots**.

A scoped slot lets the child component pass **data to the slot content** provided by the parent.

Let's take a practical example. You have a list component that renders items using a slot, but you want the parent to control how each item looks.

```
<!-- ItemList.vue -->
<template>
  <ul>
    <li v-for="item in items" :key="item.id">
      <slot :item="item" />
    </li>
  </ul>
</template>

<script setup>
defineProps({
  items: Array
})
</script>
```

Now use it like this in the parent:

```
<ItemList :items="products">
  <template #default="{ item }">
    <strong>{{ item.name }}</strong> - ${{
item.price }}
  </template>
</ItemList>

<script setup>
const products = [
  { id: 1, name: 'Phone', price: 499 },
  { id: 2, name: 'Laptop', price: 999 },
]
</script>
```

This gives the parent full control over the presentation of each item, while the ItemList handles structure and iteration.

Scoped slots are commonly used for:

Rendering dynamic lists

Data tables

Custom dropdowns

Components that accept templates for flexibility

The key takeaway is that **the child owns the data, but the parent owns the layout**.

Real-World Example: Modal Component with Slots

Let's create a BaseModal.vue component that uses multiple slots:

```
<template>
  <div class="backdrop" @click.self="close">
    <div class="modal">
      <header>
        <slot name="title">Untitled Modal</slot>
      </header>

      <main>
```

```
      <slot />
    </main>

    <footer>
      <slot name="footer">
        <button @click="close">Close</button>
      </slot>
    </footer>
  </div>
  </div>
</template>

<script setup>
const emit = defineEmits(['close'])

const close = () => {
  emit('close')
}
</script>

<style scoped>
.backdrop {
  position: fixed;
  top: 0;
  left: 0;
  right: 0;
  bottom: 0;
  background: rgba(0,0,0,0.5);
  display: flex;
  align-items: center;
  justify-content: center;
}
.modal {
  background: white;
  padding: 1.5rem;
  border-radius: 6px;
  width: 400px;
  max-width: 90vw;
}
</style>
```

Now use it like this:

```
<BaseModal @close="isModalOpen = false">
  <template #title>
    <h2>Delete Item</h2>
  </template>

  <p>Are you sure you want to delete this item?</p>

  <template #footer>
    <button @click="isModalOpen =
false">Cancel</button>
    <button @click="confirmDelete">Delete</button>
  </template>
</BaseModal>
```

The modal becomes a **reusable container** for any kind of dialog. The parent decides what the modal says, how it looks, and what actions are available.

The slot system allows maximum flexibility while keeping the component reusable and maintainable.

Final Exercise: Build a Dropdown with Scoped Slot Items

Let's create a reusable dropdown component that:

Accepts a list of items

Emits the selected item

Lets the parent customize how each item looks

```
<!-- DropdownList.vue -->
<template>
  <ul class="dropdown">
    <li
      v-for="item in items"
      :key="item.id"
      @click="$emit('select', item)"
    >
      <slot :item="item">{{ item.label }}</slot>
    </li>
  </ul>
</template>

<script setup>
```

```
defineProps({ items: Array })
defineEmits(['select'])
</script>

<style scoped>
.dropdown {
  list-style: none;
  padding: 0;
  margin: 0;
  border: 1px solid #ccc;
}
.dropdown li {
  padding: 0.5rem 1rem;
  cursor: pointer;
}
.dropdown li:hover {
  background-color: #f5f5f5;
}
</style>
Use it like this:
<DropdownList :items="users" @select="selectUser">
  <template #default="{ item }">
    <span>{{ item.name }} ({{ item.email }})</span>
  </template>
</DropdownList>

<script setup>
const users = [
  { id: 1, name: 'Ava', email: 'ava@example.com' },
  { id: 2, name: 'Daniel', email: 'daniel@example.com' }
]

const selectUser = (user) => {
  alert(`Selected: ${user.name}`)
}
</script>
```

You now have a dropdown that works across your app, renders items dynamically, and lets parents decide how to display them. This is the power of content distribution through scoped slots.

Slots in Vue give you the tools to build flexible, component-based systems without sacrificing reusability or structure. They let you:

Keep layout and structure inside the component

Let parents define the content and behavior

Build components that adapt to many contexts with zero duplication

Default slots give you a simple way to inject content. Named slots add structure. Scoped slots give you flexibility and control over rendering.

Together, they allow you to write truly reusable, maintainable, and elegant Vue components.

Component Lifecycle in Vue 3

Every Vue component goes through a predictable set of stages:

It's created and initialized.

It's mounted into the DOM.

It's updated when reactive data changes.

It's eventually unmounted and cleaned up.

At each stage, Vue provides **hooks**—functions that you can register in your component to run logic at that moment. With the Composition API, these hooks are imported from `vue` and used like any other function in your `<script setup>` block.

Here's the list of commonly used lifecycle hooks in Vue 3:

`onBeforeMount`

`onMounted`

`onBeforeUpdate`

`onUpdated`

`onBeforeUnmount`

`onUnmounted`

Each one runs at a specific point in the component's lifecycle. Let's look at them individually with detailed examples.

onMounted(): When the Component Is in the DOM

This is the most frequently used lifecycle hook. It runs **once**, right after the component has been inserted into the actual DOM. If you need to fetch data from an API, initialize a third-party library, or measure elements in the DOM, `onMounted()` is the right place.

```
<script setup>
import { ref, onMounted } from 'vue'

const data = ref(null)

onMounted(async () => {
  const res = await
fetch('https://api.example.com/data')
  data.value = await res.json()
})
</script>

<template>
  <div>
    <p v-if="!data">Loading...</p>
    <pre v-else>{{ data }}</pre>
  </div>
</template>
```

When the component mounts, the async function runs, fetches data, and updates the reactive state. Vue automatically tracks this change and updates the DOM.

This is a typical pattern in real-world apps—loading a user profile, fetching a product list, or initializing a chart or map.

onBeforeMount(): Before the Component Renders

This hook runs **right before** the component is mounted to the DOM. At this point, the component instance is created, and props and setup logic are resolved, but nothing is rendered yet.

```
<script setup>
import { onBeforeMount } from 'vue'
```

```
onBeforeMount(() => {
  console.log('Component is about to mount')
})
</script>
```

In most cases, you won't need this hook unless you're debugging or performing some low-level preparation. DOM elements are not available yet, so you can't access them here.

onBeforeUpdate() and onUpdated(): When Reactive Data Changes

When your reactive state changes, Vue re-renders the component. If you want to run code **before or after** that update, these hooks are what you need.

Let's say you want to log something before and after a reactive update:

```
<script setup>
import { ref, onBeforeUpdate, onUpdated } from 'vue'

const count = ref(0)

onBeforeUpdate(() => {
  console.log('Component is about to update')
})

onUpdated(() => {
  console.log('Component has updated')
})
</script>

<template>
  <button @click="count++">Count is {{ count }}</button>
</template>
```

When the user clicks the button, the count value changes, the component updates, and both lifecycle hooks run—one before and one after the DOM is patched.

These hooks are especially useful when integrating with non-Vue libraries that depend on the DOM layout or when optimizing re-renders.

onUnmounted(): Clean Up When the Component Is Removed

Vue runs this hook **when the component is destroyed**, meaning it's removed from the DOM and Vue stops tracking its reactivity. If your component starts any process that persists outside the component—like an interval, event listener, or WebSocket—it's critical to clean it up here.

Let's walk through a real use case: a component that starts a timer when mounted and needs to clear it on unmount.

```
<script setup>
import { ref, onMounted, onUnmounted } from 'vue'

const time = ref(0)
let timer = null

onMounted(() => {
  timer = setInterval(() => {
    time.value++
  }, 1000)
})

onUnmounted(() => {
  clearInterval(timer)
  console.log('Timer cleared')
})
</script>

<template>
  <p>Timer: {{ time }}s</p>
</template>
```

When the component is removed from the page—for example, when changing routes or toggling a `v-if`—the interval is cleared. This avoids memory leaks, double intervals, or unexpected behavior.

onBeforeUnmount(): Last Chance Before Destruction

If you need to perform cleanup **just before** the component is unmounted, but while it's still in the DOM, use `onBeforeUnmount()`.

This is rarely needed in most applications but can be helpful when:

Informing a service that a user is leaving a section

Saving unsaved form data

Warning the user about unsaved changes

```
<script setup>
import { onBeforeUnmount } from 'vue'

onBeforeUnmount(() => {
  console.log('Component is about to be destroyed')
})
</script>
```

Use this with caution, and only when necessary—especially in UI components that need to communicate with the outside world.

A Complete Example: Search Box with API Call and Cleanup

Let's say you have a search input that triggers an API call on typing. You want to:

Initialize the input on mount

Debounce input changes to avoid flooding the server

Clean up the debounce timer when the component is destroyed

Here's how that would look:

```
<script setup>
import { ref, onMounted, onUnmounted } from 'vue'

const query = ref('')
const results = ref([])
let debounceTimer = null

const fetchResults = async (term) => {
  const res = await
fetch(`https://api.example.com/search?q=${term}`)
```

```
    results.value = await res.json()
}

const onInput = (e) => {
  clearTimeout(debounceTimer)
  debounceTimer = setTimeout(() => {
    fetchResults(e.target.value)
  }, 300)
}

onMounted(() => {
  console.log('Search component mounted')
})

onUnmounted(() => {
  clearTimeout(debounceTimer)
})
</script>

<template>
  <input type="text" v-model="query"
@input="onInput" placeholder="Search..." />
  <ul>
    <li v-for="result in results"
:key="result.id">{{ result.title }}</li>
  </ul>
</template>
```

This example combines reactive data, an external API call, debounce logic, and cleanup—demonstrating how lifecycle hooks support real workflows and performance considerations.

When You Should Use Lifecycle Hooks

onMounted: when you need to interact with the DOM, load data, or set up services

onUnmounted: when you need to clear timers, listeners, or external subscriptions

onUpdated: when you need to respond to DOM changes caused by reactive state

`onBeforeMount`, `onBeforeUpdate`, `onBeforeUnmount`: when timing is critical for preparation or cleanup

You won't always need every hook in every component, but when you do need them, using them correctly is critical to stability and performance.

Lifecycle hooks in Vue 3 are simple but powerful. They allow your component to behave intelligently at each stage of its existence, and they give you full control over side effects.

Used correctly, they:

Prevent memory leaks

Improve user experience

Keep logic scoped to the component

Help manage external services, APIs, and libraries cleanly

By mastering these hooks, you give your Vue components the ability to not just render data reactively, but behave responsibly and cleanly throughout their lifespan.

Start with Intentional Folder Grouping

A scalable component structure starts with asking: *what kind of component is this?*

In most Vue apps, you'll find four major categories:

Base (UI primitives) – Generic building blocks like buttons, inputs, modals, and cards that don't contain app-specific logic.

Layout (structural wrappers) – Containers that define the layout of your application, such as headers, sidebars, navbars, and layout templates.

Feature (functional or domain-specific) – Components tied to business logic or application-specific features. Think of user profile forms, order lists, dashboards, etc.

Page (route-level views) – Top-level components that map directly to routes and typically orchestrate multiple feature and layout components.

Here's a practical folder structure based on those ideas:

```
src/
├── components/
│   ├── base/
│   ├── layout/
│   ├── features/
│   │   ├── auth/
│   │   ├── users/
│   │   └── products/
│   └── shared/
├── pages/
├── composables/
├── assets/
├── router/
└── App.vue
```

Let's look at how each part plays a role.

Base Components: Your App's Visual Vocabulary

Base components are designed to be reused across your entire app. They should be generic and consistent. These are your **atomic UI elements**: buttons, inputs, selects, switches, loaders, and other purely presentational components.

Each one should ideally follow these guidelines:

Accept props to control behavior

Emit standard events

Be style-consistent

Avoid business logic or application-specific references

Example: `BaseButton.vue`

```
<template>
  <button
    :class="['base-button', { disabled }]"
    :disabled="disabled"
    @click="$emit('click')"
  >
    <slot />
  </button>
</template>

<script setup>
defineProps({
  disabled: Boolean
})
defineEmits(['click'])
</script>

<style scoped>
.base-button {
  padding: 0.5rem 1.2rem;
  background-color: #007bff;
  color: white;
  border: none;
  border-radius: 4px;
}
.disabled {
  background-color: #ccc;
  cursor: not-allowed;
}
</style>
```

This component can be used anywhere—from login forms to admin panels—without modification.

Prefixing with `Base` is a convention that signals: *this component has no domain-specific logic*. It's reusable everywhere.

115

Layout Components: Wrapping the Page

Layout components are responsible for structure, not content. They define how elements are arranged visually. For example, a main layout might include a header, a sidebar, and a slot for page content.

Example: `AppLayout.vue`

```
<template>
  <div class="layout">
    <Sidebar />
    <div class="main">
      <Header />
      <slot />
    </div>
  </div>
</template>

<script setup>
import Sidebar from './Sidebar.vue'
import Header from './Header.vue'
</script>
```

These components help you avoid duplication. Without layout components, you'd end up repeating `<Header>` and `<Sidebar>` in every page. Keeping layout centralized also makes it easier to change the structure globally.

Feature Components: Encapsulating Business Logic

Feature components are tied to a specific part of your application's functionality. They aren't generic—they know about your app's domain. For example, `UserList.vue`, `ProductForm.vue`, `InvoiceSummary.vue`.

To keep things organized, group related feature components into folders based on the domain or module:

```
components/
  features/
    auth/
      LoginForm.vue
      RegisterForm.vue
    users/
      UserList.vue
```

```
      UserProfile.vue
    products/
      ProductCard.vue
      ProductForm.vue
```

Each of these components may contain their own internal state, validation logic, or calls to external services. They are specific to their context, and you usually don't reuse them outside that domain.

Keeping your features grouped makes it easy to find related components, onboard new team members, and scale features independently.

Page Components: Top-Level Views

In Vue Router, each route typically loads a **page component**. These are often found in a `pages/` folder and are responsible for:

Assembling layout and feature components

Coordinating data loading (e.g., calling API endpoints)

Managing page-level state

A page component should **not** contain base components directly unless necessary. Instead, it composes the page using existing features.

Example: `pages/UserDashboard.vue`

```
<template>
  <AppLayout>
    <UserProfile :user="user" />
    <UserActivity :logs="logs" />
  </AppLayout>
</template>

<script setup>
import UserProfile from
'@/components/features/users/UserProfile.vue'
import UserActivity from
'@/components/features/users/UserActivity.vue'
import AppLayout from
'@/components/layout/AppLayout.vue'
```

```
const user = { name: 'Amina', email:
'amina@example.com' }
const logs = [/* activity logs here */]
</script>
```

This component brings everything together but doesn't define the low-level details—that's handled by its child components.

Shared Components: Bridging Features

Not all components are entirely generic or specific to one feature. Some components fall somewhere in between—they're **shared across features**, but not generic enough to be `base/`.

Think of `NotificationBanner.vue`, `UserAvatar.vue`, `TagLabel.vue`, or `EmptyState.vue`.

To avoid mixing them with either base or feature components, it's often helpful to create a `shared/` folder:

```
components/
  shared/
    NotificationBanner.vue
    EmptyState.vue
    SectionTitle.vue
```

These components typically:

Are visual or functional helpers

Can be reused across multiple features

Don't include layout or routing logic

Component Naming Conventions

Consistent naming helps developers quickly identify what a component is for and where it fits.

Use names that reflect both **function and scope**:

`BaseButton.vue` — generic UI button

`UserProfile.vue` — feature-specific profile display

118

`AppLayout.vue` — layout for pages

`ProductForm.vue` — form tied to a specific domain

`LoginForm.vue` — scoped to the auth feature

Avoid abbreviations unless widely understood. Clear, descriptive names make codebases more readable and searchable.

Tips for Maintaining Scalable Component Architecture

Start with clear boundaries. Don't wait until your `components/` folder has 100 files to start organizing.

Group by responsibility, not just file type. Pages, features, layout, and base components all serve different purposes.

Avoid deep nesting. A folder depth of 2 or 3 is usually sufficient. Deeper nesting makes navigation and imports harder.

Use PascalCase for filenames. Vue automatically registers components in PascalCase. Keeping filenames consistent avoids confusion.

Avoid duplication. If you copy and paste a component more than once, it's time to refactor and extract a reusable version.

Document your structure. Especially on teams, having a short `README.md` or `architecture.md` explaining the component strategy helps everyone stay aligned.

Organizing your components well from the start—or refactoring them early—is one of the highest-leverage things you can do for a Vue project. It improves collaboration, reduces friction when scaling features, and makes the codebase more approachable.

Vue doesn't enforce a strict structure, but it gives you the flexibility to define one that reflects the shape and needs of your application. The key is consistency and clarity—every component should have a clear place, a clear purpose, and a clear boundary.

Chapter 5: Composition API Deep Dive

Vue 3 introduced the **Composition API** as a new way to organize component logic. Compared to the Options API—which grouped code by *option types* (`data`, `methods`, `computed`, etc.)—the Composition API groups logic by *feature*. This makes it easier to structure larger components, extract reusable logic, and create cleaner mental models.

So far, you've already been using the Composition API through `<script setup>` and functions like `ref`, `reactive`, and `computed`. In this chapter, we'll go deeper into the tools available and how they all fit together.

What is the `setup()` Function?

In Vue 3's Composition API, `setup()` is the **entry point** for a component's logic. Vue calls this function **before** the component is created, and whatever you return from `setup()` is exposed to your component's template.

Inside `setup()`, you can:

Declare reactive state (`ref`, `reactive`)

Define methods and computed properties

Use lifecycle hooks

Access component props

Use or define composables

If you're using the `<script setup>` syntax (which is strongly recommended), you don't have to manually declare a `setup()` function—Vue automatically wraps your code in one for you behind the scenes.

But whether you're writing it explicitly or implicitly with `<script setup>`, the core behavior is the same.

Basic Use of `setup()`

Here's a simple Vue component using the standard Composition API syntax with an explicit `setup()` function.

```
<script>
import { ref } from 'vue'

export default {
  setup() {
    const count = ref(0)

    const increment = () => {
      count.value++
    }

    return {
      count,
      increment
    }
  }
}
</script>

<template>
  <button @click="increment">Count: {{ count
}}</button>
</template>
```

In this example:

`count` is a reactive reference initialized to 0

`increment()` is a method that updates that state

Returning `count` and `increment` from `setup()` makes them available to the template

Everything you want to use in your template must be returned from `setup()`.

The `<script setup>` Syntax

Now let's write the same component using `<script setup>`, which is the recommended approach in Vue 3.

```
<script setup>
import { ref } from 'vue'

const count = ref(0)

const increment = () => {
  count.value++
}
</script>

<template>
  <button @click="increment">Count: {{ count }}</button>
</template>
```

With `<script setup>`, Vue automatically handles the `setup()` function for you. You don't need to return anything. All variables declared in this block are directly usable in the template. This makes your code cleaner and more maintainable, especially as components grow in size.

Accessing Props and Emits in `setup()`

You can use `setup()` to access props and emit events. When using `<script setup>`, this becomes even easier with `defineProps()` and `defineEmits()`.

Example:

```
<!-- Message.vue -->
<script setup>
const props = defineProps({
  message: String
})

const emit = defineEmits(['close'])

const close = () => {
  emit('close')
}
</script>
```

```
<template>
  <div class="alert">
    <span>{{ message }}</span>
    <button @click="close">×</button>
  </div>
</template>
```

Here, `defineProps()` tells Vue which props this component expects. `defineEmits()` defines the custom events this component might emit. These are both compile-time macros that let you skip boilerplate code.

The parent can use the component like this:

```
<Message message="Hello!" @close="handleClose" />
```

This is the Composition API's preferred way of working with props and events.

Lifecycle Hooks in `setup()`

In Vue 3, all lifecycle hooks are used directly inside `setup()` using functions imported from `vue`.

For example, if you want to run code after the component is mounted:

```
<script setup>
import { ref, onMounted } from 'vue'

const user = ref(null)

onMounted(async () => {
  const res = await fetch('/api/user')
  user.value = await res.json()
})
</script>

<template>
  <div v-if="user">Hello, {{ user.name }}</div>
  <div v-else>Loading...</div>
</template>
```

This is a common pattern: define state using `ref()`, fetch data in `onMounted()`, and display a loading message until the data arrives.

Other available hooks:

```
onBeforeMount

onUpdated

onBeforeUnmount

onUnmounted

onErrorCaptured

onRenderTracked

onRenderTriggered
```

You can use any of these inside `setup()` or `<script setup>`.

Why `setup()` Improves Logic Grouping

In the Options API, you define state in `data()`, methods in `methods`, computed properties in `computed`, and so on. This splits up related logic across different blocks, which becomes harder to manage in large components.

With `setup()`, you define everything together by purpose.

Take a look at this small example of form handling:

```
<script setup>
import { ref, computed } from 'vue'

const firstName = ref('')
const lastName = ref('')

const fullName = computed(() => `${firstName.value}
${lastName.value}`)

const reset = () => {
  firstName.value = ''
  lastName.value = ''
}
</script>

<template>
  <input v-model="firstName" placeholder="First
name" />
```

```
  <input v-model="lastName" placeholder="Last name"
/>
  <p>Full name: {{ fullName }}</p>
  <button @click="reset">Reset</button>
</template>
```

Everything related to the form is declared together—state, derived state, and actions. This makes your logic easier to understand and reuse.

Returning Values from setup()

In classic `setup()` syntax, if you want your data, methods, or computed properties to be available in the template, you must **return them explicitly**.

```
return {
  count,
  increment
}
```

If you forget to return a variable, Vue won't know about it in the template, and you'll get an undefined error.

With `<script setup>`, all top-level variables and functions are automatically exposed to the template. No return is needed.

If you're using a regular `setup()` and want to expose logic only to other composables or internal code—not the template—you can return selectively. Or return nothing at all if the component is headless (e.g., provides a service only).

Exercise: Timer Component with Start and Stop

Let's bring everything together into a full component example that uses:

`setup()` (via `<script setup>`)

`ref` for reactive state

event handling

lifecycle cleanup

```
<script setup>
import { ref, onMounted, onUnmounted } from 'vue'
```

125

```
const time = ref(0)
let interval = null

const start = () => {
  if (!interval) {
    interval = setInterval(() => {
      time.value++
    }, 1000)
  }
}

const stop = () => {
  clearInterval(interval)
  interval = null
}

onUnmounted(() => {
  clearInterval(interval)
})
</script>

<template>
  <p>Time: {{ time }}s</p>
  <button @click="start">Start</button>
  <button @click="stop">Stop</button>
</template>
```

This is a complete, functional component. When mounted, it waits for the user to start the timer. The interval updates reactive state, and the `onUnmounted()` hook ensures that timers are cleaned up to avoid memory leaks.

The `setup()` function is the foundation of every Vue 3 component built with the Composition API. It gives you control over state, logic, lifecycle, and how your component communicates with the rest of the application—all within a single, predictable structure.

When you understand `setup()`, you gain the ability to:

Build components with scoped and reusable logic

Group code naturally by feature, not syntax

Compose small, testable units of behavior with composables

Transition from Options API to Composition API smoothly and confidently

In the next section, we'll go further into Vue's reactivity system and look more closely at how `ref`, `reactive`, `computed`, and `watch` work together to create responsive, powerful interfaces.

Creating Reactive Values with ref()

When you need to store and reactively update a **single value**—such as a string, number, boolean, array, or object—the most straightforward approach is to use `ref()`.

Here's a basic example:

```
<script setup>
import { ref } from 'vue'

const count = ref(0)

const increment = () => {
  count.value++
}
</script>

<template>
  <button @click="increment">Count: {{ count }}</button>
</template>
```

When you declare `const count = ref(0)`, Vue wraps the value in a **reactive reference object** with a `.value` property. That `.value` is what you read or write inside your JavaScript logic.

However, inside templates, Vue **automatically unwraps** refs for you—so you can use `count` directly, without `.value`.

This distinction is important:

In JavaScript: `count.value`

In the template: `{{ count }}` or `v-bind="count"`

This unwrapping behavior only works inside templates. If you're accessing a ref in another function or composable, always use `.value`.

Real example: simple form input

```
<script setup>
import { ref } from 'vue'

const name = ref('')
</script>

<template>
  <input v-model="name" placeholder="Enter your name" />
  <p>Your name is: {{ name }}</p>
</template>
```

This creates a two-way binding with the input and a reactive text display. Every keystroke updates the ref, and the DOM reflects the change automatically.

Creating Reactive Objects with `reactive()`

While `ref()` is excellent for primitives or a single value, `reactive()` is better when you need a **structured object** with multiple related properties.

Here's a simple user profile:

```
<script setup>
import { reactive } from 'vue'

const user = reactive({
  name: 'Amina',
  email: 'amina@example.com',
  isAdmin: false
})
</script>

<template>
  <h2>{{ user.name }}</h2>
  <p>Email: {{ user.email }}</p>
```

```
  <p v-if="user.isAdmin">Administrator Access</p>
</template>
```

The `reactive()` function returns a **deep reactive proxy**. This means Vue tracks every property and sub-property within the object, and updates the DOM accordingly when any of them change.

There's no `.value` here—just direct access to the properties.

```
user.name = 'Daniel'    // triggers reactivity
```

This pattern is especially useful for form models, user profiles, configuration objects, and nested data structures.

Derived State with `computed()`

Sometimes you need to display or act on a value that's based on other reactive values. Instead of manually recalculating that derived value, you can use a **computed property**.

Here's a case where `computed()` makes sense:

```
<script setup>
import { ref, computed } from 'vue'

const firstName = ref('Ada')
const lastName = ref('Lovelace')

const fullName = computed(() => `${firstName.value}
${lastName.value}`)
</script>

<template>
  <p>Full Name: {{ fullName }}</p>
</template>
```

When either `firstName` or `lastName` changes, `fullName` will automatically re-evaluate. Vue caches the result and only recalculates when its dependencies change.

`computed()` is **reactive and memoized**. Use it when:

You want to calculate something based on other reactive data

129

The result is intended for display or use in templates

You don't want unnecessary recalculations

You can even use `computed()` with `reactive()`:

```
const user = reactive({ first: 'Ava', last: 'Carter' })

const initials = computed(() => {
  return `${user.first[0]}.${user.last[0]}.`
})
```

This keeps your logic declarative and organized.

Watching Changes with `watch()`

While `computed()` is for **declaring a derived value**, `watch()` is for **performing side effects** when a value changes. A side effect might be:

Sending an API request

Writing to localStorage

Logging a message

Triggering an animation or scroll

Here's a basic example:

```
<script setup>
import { ref, watch } from 'vue'

const searchTerm = ref('')

watch(searchTerm, (newValue, oldValue) => {
  console.log(`Search term changed from
"${oldValue}" to "${newValue}"`)
})
</script>

<template>
  <input v-model="searchTerm"
placeholder="Search..." />
</template>
```

Every time `searchTerm` changes, the watcher runs. You get access to both the new and old value.

You can also use the third parameter to customize behavior:

```
watch(searchTerm, fetchResults, { immediate: true })
```

This makes the watcher run immediately on component setup, not just on change.

Watching reactive objects

If you want to watch a **reactive object**, like one created with `reactive()`, you need to pass a getter function to `watch()`.

```
watch(
  () => user.name,
  (newName) => {
    console.log('User name changed:', newName)
  }
)
```

If you want to watch the entire object (including nested values), you can use the `deep` option:

```
watch(user, () => {
  console.log('User object changed')
}, { deep: true })
```

Use this carefully—deep watching can be expensive if the object is large.

Choosing Between `ref()` and `reactive()`

This is one of the most common questions developers have when learning the Composition API.

Use `ref()` when:

You're tracking a primitive (number, string, boolean)

You want to store a DOM element (e.g., `ref(null)` and `v-bind="el"`)

You need `.value` for consistent access (especially outside templates)

Use `reactive()` when:

You're working with an object or array with multiple properties

You want to access fields without `.value`

You're modeling structured data like forms, settings, or user info

If needed, you can mix them:

```
const form = reactive({ email: '', password: '' })
const isSubmitting = ref(false)
```

You'll find yourself combining `ref`, `reactive`, and `computed` often in real applications.

Exercise: Reactive Form with Computed Summary

Let's build a real component that brings everything together:

```
<script setup>
import { reactive, computed, watch } from 'vue'

const form = reactive({
  firstName: '',
  lastName: '',
  subscribed: false
})

const fullName = computed(() => {
  return `${form.firstName}
${form.lastName}`.trim()
})

watch(() => form.subscribed, (newVal) => {
  if (newVal) {
    console.log(`${fullName.value} subscribed to
updates`)
  }
})
</script>

<template>
  <form>
```

```
    <input v-model="form.firstName"
placeholder="First Name" />
    <input v-model="form.lastName"
placeholder="Last Name" />

    <label>
      <input type="checkbox" v-
model="form.subscribed" />
      Subscribe to updates
    </label>

    <p><strong>Full Name:</strong> {{ fullName
}}</p>
  </form>
</template>
```

This form:

Uses `reactive()` to manage structured input data

Uses `computed()` to create a derived display value

Uses `watch()` to log a message when the checkbox is toggled

Everything stays reactive. The user input is reflected immediately in the display and triggers side effects only when needed.

Vue's reactivity system is precise, intuitive, and powerful once you understand how its core primitives work. Mastering `ref`, `reactive`, `computed`, and `watch` allows you to:

Model and update state clearly

Display derived values without extra logic

Run side effects at the right time

Keep your components clean, efficient, and scalable

There's no magic involved. Vue simply tracks what values are used and automatically schedules DOM updates and effects when they change. Your job is to declare the relationships between data, behavior, and side effects.

What Is a Composable?

In Vue 3, a composable is simply a **function** that encapsulates some reactive logic and returns the data, methods, or computed properties needed by a component.

This is what makes the Composition API so flexible. Instead of putting all logic inside a component's `<script setup>` block or `setup()` function, you move parts of it into a regular JavaScript function that you can import and reuse anywhere.

A composable:

Can use Vue's reactivity APIs (`ref`, `reactive`, `computed`, `watch`, etc.)

Can use lifecycle hooks like `onMounted()`, `onUnmounted()`, etc.

Returns data or behavior that other components can consume

You name them with a `use` prefix by convention, such as `useMouse`, `useForm`, `useAuth`, or `useCountdown`. This helps differentiate them from components and makes their purpose clear.

Basic Example: useCounter

Let's create a basic counter logic as a composable.

Create a file called `useCounter.js` (or `.ts` if you're using TypeScript):

```js
// composables/useCounter.js
import { ref } from 'vue'

export function useCounter(initial = 0) {
  const count = ref(initial)

  const increment = () => count.value++
  const decrement = () => count.value--
  const reset = () => count.value = initial

  return {
    count,
    increment,
```

134

```
    decrement,
    reset
  }
}
```

Now, in any component, you can use this like so:

```
<script setup>
import { useCounter } from
'@/composables/useCounter'

const { count, increment, decrement, reset } =
useCounter(10)
</script>

<template>
  <div>
    <p>Count: {{ count }}</p>
    <button @click="increment">+</button>
    <button @click="decrement">-</button>
    <button @click="reset">Reset</button>
  </div>
</template>
```

This component doesn't know how the counter logic works—it simply uses it. That's the strength of composables. Logic is encapsulated, focused, and testable.

What makes composables different from ordinary JavaScript functions is that they **retain Vue's reactivity**. When you return a `ref`, `reactive` object, or `computed` from a composable, and bind it to a template, it behaves as if it was defined inside the component.

There's no special magic or syntax—just ordinary JavaScript functions working with Vue's reactive system.

Using Lifecycle Hooks Inside Composables

Composables can also use lifecycle hooks like `onMounted`, `onUnmounted`, `onUpdated`, and so on. This is particularly useful when the logic needs to react to the component's lifecycle without being tied to the component's structure.

Here's an example of a composable that tracks the mouse position:

```js
// composables/useMouse.js
import { ref, onMounted, onUnmounted } from 'vue'

export function useMouse() {
  const x = ref(0)
  const y = ref(0)

  const update = (e) => {
    x.value = e.clientX
    y.value = e.clientY
  }

  onMounted(() =>
window.addEventListener('mousemove', update))
  onUnmounted(() =>
window.removeEventListener('mousemove', update))

  return { x, y }
}
```

Use it in any component:

```vue
<script setup>
import { useMouse } from '@/composables/useMouse'

const { x, y } = useMouse()
</script>

<template>
  <p>Mouse at: {{ x }}, {{ y }}</p>
</template>
```

This composable has internal state and lifecycle management, but from the component's point of view, it behaves just like a simple reactive data source.

Sharing Behavior Without Components

Before Vue 3, the main way to reuse logic was with mixins or higher-order components. Both had significant drawbacks:

Mixins had name collisions and implicit dependencies.

Higher-order components complicated the component hierarchy.

Composables solve these problems cleanly:

No name collisions—everything is explicitly scoped inside the composable.

No hidden dependencies—you import and use only what you need.

No need to modify component inheritance or structure.

Real Example: useLocalStorage

Let's create a composable that reads and writes reactive data to `localStorage`.

```
// composables/useLocalStorage.js
import { ref, watch } from 'vue'

export function useLocalStorage(key, defaultValue)
{
  const storedValue = localStorage.getItem(key)
  const data = ref(storedValue ?
JSON.parse(storedValue) : defaultValue)

  watch(data, (newValue) => {
    localStorage.setItem(key,
JSON.stringify(newValue))
  }, { deep: true })

  return data
}
```

Usage:

```
<script setup>
import { useLocalStorage } from
'@/composables/useLocalStorage'

const theme = useLocalStorage('theme', 'light')
</script>

<template>
  <select v-model="theme">
    <option value="light">Light</option>
```

137

```
      <option value="dark">Dark</option>
    </select>
</template>
```

Now your app automatically stores and retrieves the selected theme without having to write this logic in every component.

Reusable Form Logic with Composables

You'll often find yourself writing the same logic for handling forms: defining fields, tracking validity, submitting data, and resetting. Let's extract that into a composable.

```
// composables/useForm.js
import { reactive } from 'vue'

export function useForm(initial = {}) {
  const form = reactive({ ...initial })

  const reset = () => {
    for (const key in initial) {
      form[key] = initial[key]
    }
  }

  return { form, reset }
}
```

Use it like this:

```
<script setup>
import { useForm } from '@/composables/useForm'

const { form, reset } = useForm({
  email: '',
  password: ''
})

const submit = () => {
  console.log('Form submitted:', form)
  reset()
}
</script>
```

```
<template>
  <form @submit.prevent="submit">
    <input v-model="form.email" type="email"
placeholder="Email" />
    <input v-model="form.password" type="password"
placeholder="Password" />
    <button type="submit">Login</button>
  </form>
</template>
```

This composable could be extended with:

Validation rules

Submit handlers

Field-specific status tracking

And used across multiple forms in different parts of your application.

Tips for Writing Better Composables

Use clear names: Prefix with `use` and name according to behavior (`useTheme`, `usePagination`, `useNotifications`)

Encapsulate one responsibility: Don't cram multiple unrelated concerns into one composable.

Return only what's needed: Expose minimal reactive state and methods to keep things focused.

Don't mutate external state inside the composable: Let the consumer decide how to use the data you expose.

Keep them composable: You can even use one composable inside another to build up complex behaviors.

Composables are one of the most valuable tools Vue 3 gives you. They allow you to:

Write logic once and reuse it across many components

Keep your components smaller, cleaner, and more focused

Encapsulate features without relying on inheritance or duplication

Share behavior and data without forcing a specific UI structure

The Composition API gives you the primitives (`ref`, `reactive`, `watch`, `computed`, lifecycle hooks), and composables are how you organize and scale them across your application.

As you build larger apps, composables will become essential for maintaining quality, testability, and development speed.

Understanding *provide* and *inject*

In Vue, `provide` and `inject` work together as a **pair**:

A component **provides** a value using `provide()`.

Any **descendant component**, regardless of how many levels deep, can **inject** that value using `inject()`.

The data flows from a provider down the component tree, but without explicitly passing it through props. This works even if there are several intermediate components in between that don't use the data.

This pattern is particularly useful when:

You need to share global context (like theme, auth status, locale)

You want to provide services (like a reusable API or store)

You need to keep intermediate components simple and unaware of global context

The Basics: How to Use **provide and inject**

Let's go through the simplest possible example. We'll have a parent component provide a string value, and a nested child inject and use it.

Provider Component

```
<!-- App.vue -->
<script setup>
```

```
import { provide } from 'vue'
import MessageDisplay from
'./components/MessageDisplay.vue'

provide('appMessage', 'Hello from parent!')
</script>

<template>
  <div>
    <h1>Main App</h1>
    <MessageDisplay />
  </div>
</template>
```

Consumer Component

```
<!-- MessageDisplay.vue -->
<script setup>
import { inject } from 'vue'

const appMessage = inject('appMessage', 'Default
fallback message')
</script>

<template>
  <p>Injected Message: {{ appMessage }}</p>
</template>
```

Here's what's happening:

The `App.vue` component uses `provide()` to make a string (`'Hello from parent!'`) available under the key `'appMessage'`.

The `MessageDisplay.vue` component injects this value using the same key.

Even though there's no direct prop passing, the value is shared and reactive.

Note: The second argument to `inject()` is a default value. If the key is not found, Vue uses this fallback.

Using Reactive Values with `provide` and `inject`

In most real-world cases, you'll want to provide **reactive state**, not just static values. Vue supports this perfectly—simply provide a `ref`, `reactive`, or `computed` value, and the consumer will receive it as-is.

Provider with a `ref`

```
<!-- App.vue -->
<script setup>
import { provide, ref } from 'vue'
import Sidebar from './components/Sidebar.vue'

const theme = ref('light')

provide('theme', theme)
</script>

<template>
  <div :class="theme">
    <Sidebar />
  </div>
</template>
```

Consumer Component

```
<!-- Sidebar.vue -->
<script setup>
import { inject } from 'vue'

const theme = inject('theme')
</script>

<template>
  <p>Current Theme: {{ theme }}</p>
</template>
```

This example behaves just like if you had passed `theme` as a prop—but with less coupling. The reactive value is shared directly, and any updates to it are reflected immediately in both the provider and consumer.

Real-World Example: Providing a Service

Now let's create a more realistic example: a notification system.

We'll create a notification composable and provide it to any component that needs to trigger messages.

Create a composable

```
// composables/useNotifications.js
import { ref } from 'vue'

export function useNotifications() {
  const messages = ref([])

  const notify = (text, type = 'info') => {
    messages.value.push({ text, type, id:
Date.now() })
  }

  const clear = () => {
    messages.value = []
  }

  return { messages, notify, clear }
}
```

Provider Component

```
<!-- App.vue -->
<script setup>
import { provide } from 'vue'
import { useNotifications } from
'./composables/useNotifications'
import NotificationList from
'./components/NotificationList.vue'
import SendMessage from
'./components/SendMessage.vue'

const notificationService = useNotifications()

provide('notifyService', notificationService)
</script>

<template>
  <NotificationList />
  <SendMessage />
```

```
</template>
```

Consumer Component

```html
<!-- SendMessage.vue -->
<script setup>
import { inject } from 'vue'

const { notify } = inject('notifyService')

const send = () => {
  notify('Message sent!', 'success')
}
</script>

<template>
  <button @click="send">Send Message</button>
</template>
```

Display Notifications

```html
<!-- NotificationList.vue -->
<script setup>
import { inject } from 'vue'

const { messages, clear } = inject('notifyService')
</script>

<template>
  <div v-if="messages.length">
    <div v-for="msg in messages" :key="msg.id"
:class="msg.type">
      {{ msg.text }}
    </div>
    <button @click="clear">Clear</button>
  </div>
</template>
```

In this setup:

The App.vue provides a global notification system.

Any child component can inject and use it.

The components stay decoupled from each other and don't rely on prop-passing.

This is the kind of pattern that helps your app scale cleanly, especially as the number of components increases.

Avoiding Pitfalls

While `provide` and `inject` are powerful, you should follow a few guidelines:

Only use this pattern when **props become inconvenient or noisy**, especially across 3+ layers.

Don't overuse it. If a value is specific to a component and its direct child, **use props** instead.

Keep your keys **unique and descriptive**, especially if you're using string keys (you can also use symbols to avoid collisions).

Prefer **composables** as values you provide. This keeps logic modular and testable.

When Not to Use It

There are cases where `provide` and `inject` are not appropriate:

For one-off prop passing between parent and child—use props.

When the state is meant to be local and isolated.

When you're dealing with sibling components—use a shared parent to manage state or a store (like Pinia) for global state.

Final Exercise: Provide an Auth Context

Let's build a composable and inject it across your app to manage login state.

Auth Composable

```
// composables/useAuth.js
import { ref } from 'vue'

export function useAuth() {
  const user = ref(null)
```

```
  const login = (username) => {
    user.value = { name: username }
  }

  const logout = () => {
    user.value = null
  }

  return { user, login, logout }
}
```

App.vue

```
<script setup>
import { provide } from 'vue'
import { useAuth } from './composables/useAuth'

const auth = useAuth()
provide('auth', auth)
</script>

<template>
  <slot />
</template>
```

Header.vue

```
<script setup>
import { inject } from 'vue'

const { user, logout } = inject('auth')
</script>

<template>
  <div v-if="user">
    <span>Welcome, {{ user.name }}</span>
    <button @click="logout">Logout</button>
  </div>
</template>
```

LoginForm.vue

```
<script setup>
import { inject, ref } from 'vue'

const { login } = inject('auth')
const username = ref('')

const submit = () => {
  login(username.value)
}
</script>

<template>
  <input v-model="username" placeholder="Username"
/>
  <button @click="submit">Login</button>
</template>
```

This pattern lets your login state be injected anywhere without passing user or login/logout functions through each level of your app manually.

provide and inject give you a clean way to share reactive state, services, or configuration across deeply nested components. They're powerful, but they should be used thoughtfully and deliberately to simplify your architecture— not to replace props entirely.

The most effective use cases include:

Global themes or locale

Application-wide services like notifications, auth, or modals

Sharing state across isolated sections of a component tree

In the next section, we'll explore **Mixing Options API with the Composition API**, which helps bridge old and new codebases and lets you incrementally adopt Composition API in legacy Vue apps.

Mixing Options API with Composition API

In Vue 3, if you're using the classic component format—with data(), methods, computed, and so on—you can add a setup() function to that same component. Everything defined inside `setup()` will work just like it does in Composition API-only components.

At runtime, Vue initializes `setup()` first, then continues to process the component using the Options API. That means:

Reactive values from `setup()` are available to the template **if you return them from `setup()`.**

Data from `data()`, computed properties, and methods declared in the Options API are also available in the template.

They do **not** automatically share state with each other unless you do so explicitly.

This separation means you can choose to gradually extract logic to `setup()` while maintaining your existing component structure.

Example: Combining `setup()` with `data()` and `methods`

Let's start with a straightforward example that shows how both APIs can live together.

```
<script>
import { ref, onMounted } from 'vue'

export default {
  name: 'MixedComponent',

  data() {
    return {
      countFromData: 10
    }
  },

  methods: {
    multiplyDataCount() {
      return this.countFromData * 2
    }
  },

  setup() {
    const count = ref(0)
```

```
    const increment = () => {
      count.value++
    }

    onMounted(() => {
      console.log('Component mounted (from setup)')
    })

    return {
      count,
      increment
    }
  },

  mounted() {
    console.log('Component mounted (from Options
API)')
  }
}
</script>

<template>
  <div>
    <p>Options API Count: {{ countFromData }} (x2 =
{{ multiplyDataCount() }})</p>
    <p>Composition API Count: {{ count }}</p>
    <button @click="increment">Increment
(Composition API)</button>
  </div>
</template>
```

Here's how this behaves:

count and increment are defined in setup() and returned to make them usable in the template.

countFromData and multiplyDataCount are classic Options API values.

Both sets of data can be used in the template at the same time.

Both onMounted() and mounted() lifecycle hooks are triggered (from Composition API and Options API respectively).

This gives you flexibility, but also means you need to be aware of **which API owns what state**.

Sharing Data Between Options API and Composition API

Reactive values from the Composition API are **not accessible inside Options API methods or lifecycle hooks,** unless you manually assign them.

Here's what will **not work**:

```
methods: {
  logCount() {
    console.log(this.count) // undefined if `count`
is from setup()
  }
}
```

If you need a Composition API value inside an Options API method, you need to either:

Move that method into `setup()` instead, or

Assign the value to a property in `data()` or `this`

Here's one safe approach to expose Composition API values to Options API code:

```
setup(props, { expose }) {
  const count = ref(0)
  expose({ count })
  return { count }
}
```

However, in practice, it's often clearer and cleaner to **keep logic defined in one API isolated**, and avoid mixing unless you need to.

Why and When You Should Mix APIs

Let's look at a few valid real-world use cases where mixing both APIs is practical and appropriate:

Case 1: Gradual Migration of Legacy Components

You have a component written entirely in the Options API, but now you want to introduce a composable or use `ref()` for new logic.

```
setup() {
  const localStorageValue = useLocalStorage('my-key', 'default')
  return { localStorageValue }
}
```

This allows you to bring in new functionality without refactoring the rest of the component.

Case 2: Using Lifecycle Hooks Not Available in Options API

Some Composition API lifecycle hooks, like `onRenderTracked()` and `onRenderTriggered()`, **do not exist** in the Options API. If you need them, you must use `setup()`.

```
setup() {
  onRenderTracked((e) => {
    console.log('Tracked:', e)
  })
}
```

This is helpful for performance debugging and reactivity diagnostics.

Case 3: Integrating with Composables or Global Services

Your app uses composables like `useAuth()` or `useTheme()` throughout the codebase, and you want to call them from an Options API component.

```
setup() {
  const { user } = useAuth()
  return { user }
}
```

This allows you to reuse logic without rewriting components entirely.

Example: Combining with Third-Party Composables

Let's say you're using a package that provides a Vue composable for working with a socket connection:

```
// composables/useSocket.js
```

```
import { ref, onUnmounted } from 'vue'

export function useSocket(url) {
  const connected = ref(false)

  const socket = new WebSocket(url)

  socket.onopen = () => (connected.value = true)
  socket.onclose = () => (connected.value = false)

  onUnmounted(() => socket.close())

  return { connected, socket }
}
```

To use it in an Options API component:

```
<script>
import { useSocket } from '@/composables/useSocket'

export default {
  setup() {
    const { connected } =
useSocket('wss://example.com/socket')
    return { connected }
  },
  data() {
    return {
      status: 'Waiting for connection...'
    }
  },
  watch: {
    connected(newVal) {
      this.status = newVal ? 'Connected' :
'Disconnected'
    }
  }
}
</script>

<template>
  <p>Status: {{ status }}</p>
</template>
```

In this case, the reactive value `connected` from `useSocket()` is returned from `setup()`, making it available to the Options API's `watch` block. This shows how the two APIs can cooperate when needed.

Guidelines for Mixing

To keep things clean and understandable:

Group related logic together—don't define part of a feature in `setup()` and part in `data()` or `methods`.

Use `setup()` primarily for new logic, composables, or third-party libraries.

Use the Options API if the component is small, or if it's mostly template logic with simple state.

Avoid name collisions between returned values from `setup()` and properties in `data()` or `methods`. Vue will prioritize returned `setup()` values.

Favor consistency across a component—if you're writing new code and the component is already using Composition API, stay within it.

Final Exercise: Mixed Component with Reactive Theme and Classic Form

Let's create a component where the theme is injected via Composition API, but the form is handled using Options API.

```
<script>
import { inject } from 'vue'

export default {
  name: 'UserForm',

  props: ['onSubmit'],

  data() {
    return {
      name: '',
      email: ''
    }
  },
```

```
  methods: {
    submitForm() {
      this.onSubmit({ name: this.name, email:
this.email })
    }
  },

  setup() {
    const theme = inject('theme', 'light')
    return { theme }
  }
}
</script>

<template>
  <div :class="theme">
    <form @submit.prevent="submitForm">
      <input v-model="name" placeholder="Name" />
      <input v-model="email" placeholder="Email" />
      <button type="submit">Send</button>
    </form>
  </div>
</template>
```

In this example:

The form logic stays in the familiar `data()` and `methods`.

The theme comes from an injected reactive value using Composition API.

The template uses both sources cleanly.

This gives you the flexibility to adopt Vue 3 features gradually and strategically.

Mixing the Options API and Composition API is completely supported in Vue 3. It's not a transitional hack, it's important to mix them with discipline. Avoid scattering logic across both APIs for the same concern. Instead, keep the logic of a feature together in one API whenever possible.

Chapter 6: Forms and User Input Handling

User input is one of the most interactive parts of any frontend application. When users fill out forms, they expect responsiveness, helpful feedback, and stability. Vue gives you robust tools to make this seamless—especially with the Composition API, where form state and logic can be grouped and reused in a clean, testable way.

Working with Forms in Vue

Handling forms in Vue is centered around reactivity and declarative syntax. Every input field—whether it's a text box, checkbox, radio button, or select dropdown—can be directly bound to a reactive variable. Vue handles the syncing between the DOM and your JavaScript logic automatically.

You don't need to manually wire up `addEventListener` or use `querySelector` to get values from inputs. Instead, Vue gives you the `v-model` directive, which creates a two-way binding between your form elements and your component's state.

Basic Text Input Form

In a basic use case, you want a form that allows a user to enter their name and email address, and you want to respond to that data when they submit.

```
<script setup>
import { ref } from 'vue'

const name = ref('')
const email = ref('')

const handleSubmit = () => {
  console.log('Name:', name.value)
  console.log('Email:', email.value)
}
</script>

<template>
```

```
  <form @submit.prevent="handleSubmit">
    <label>
      Name:
      <input type="text" v-model="name" />
    </label>

    <label>
      Email:
      <input type="email" v-model="email" />
    </label>

    <button type="submit">Submit</button>
  </form>
</template>
```

In this example:

`v-model` creates a reactive connection between the input elements and the JavaScript state.

You don't use `.value` in the template—Vue unwraps it for you.

On form submission, the `handleSubmit` function uses `.value` to access the data because you're working in JavaScript context.

There's no `document.querySelector`, no `input.value`, and no boilerplate. The state is reactive and always up to date.

Using `reactive()` for Structured Form Data

When you're handling a form with multiple fields—especially fields that logically belong together—it's often better to use `reactive()` to manage a single object instead of declaring multiple `ref()`s.

```
<script setup>
import { reactive } from 'vue'

const form = reactive({
  name: '',
  email: '',
  message: ''
})
```

```
const submit = () => {
  console.log('Submitted form:', { ...form })
}
</script>

<template>
  <form @submit.prevent="submit">
    <label>
      Name:
      <input v-model="form.name" />
    </label>

    <label>
      Email:
      <input type="email" v-model="form.email" />
    </label>

    <label>
      Message:
      <textarea v-model="form.message" />
    </label>

    <button type="submit">Send</button>
  </form>
</template>
```

This setup keeps all related fields inside a single object. It's easier to reset, validate, or manipulate the whole form this way—particularly useful when working with larger forms or reusable form logic.

You can reset the entire form like this:

form.name = ''

form.email = ''

form.message = ''

Or reset all fields dynamically:

```
Object.keys(form).forEach(key => form[key] = '')
```

Working with Checkboxes and Radios

Checkboxes and radio buttons behave slightly differently from text inputs because their values are not strings by default—they're booleans or selections from predefined options.

For checkboxes, Vue binds the `checked` state to a boolean or array depending on the structure.

Single checkbox:

```
<script setup>
import { ref } from 'vue'

const accepted = ref(false)
</script>

<template>
  <label>
    <input type="checkbox" v-model="accepted" />
    I accept the terms
  </label>

  <p v-if="accepted">Thanks for accepting.</p>
</template>
```

Multiple checkboxes (e.g. skills):

```
<script setup>
import { ref } from 'vue'

const selectedSkills = ref([])
</script>

<template>
  <label><input type="checkbox" value="JavaScript"
v-model="selectedSkills" /> JavaScript</label>
  <label><input type="checkbox" value="Vue" v-
model="selectedSkills" /> Vue</label>
  <label><input type="checkbox" value="TypeScript"
v-model="selectedSkills" /> TypeScript</label>

  <p>Selected: {{ selectedSkills }}</p>
</template>
```

In this case, Vue automatically adds or removes the selected values from the array.

Radio buttons:

```
<script setup>
import { ref } from 'vue'

const gender = ref('')
</script>

<template>
  <label><input type="radio" value="male" v-model="gender" /> Male</label>
  <label><input type="radio" value="female" v-model="gender" /> Female</label>

  <p>Selected Gender: {{ gender }}</p>
</template>
```

Here, only one radio button can be selected at a time. Vue manages this behavior automatically based on the shared `v-model`.

Select Dropdowns

Vue also supports both single and multiple select fields using `v-model`.

Single select:

```
<script setup>
import { ref } from 'vue'

const country = ref('')
</script>

<template>
  <select v-model="country">
    <option value="">Select Country</option>
    <option value="us">United States</option>
    <option value="ng">Nigeria</option>
    <option value="uk">United Kingdom</option>
  </select>
```

```
  <p>Selected: {{ country }}</p>
</template>
```

Multi-select:

```
<script setup>
import { ref } from 'vue'

const selectedLanguages = ref([])
</script>

<template>
  <select v-model="selectedLanguages" multiple>
    <option value="english">English</option>
    <option value="french">French</option>
    <option value="yoruba">Yoruba</option>
  </select>

  <p>Selected Languages: {{ selectedLanguages
}}</p>
</template>
```

When `multiple` is used, Vue automatically binds the selected values to an array.

Custom Input Components

You can also build reusable input components that support `v-model`. Vue 3 makes this very clean by supporting `modelValue` and `update:modelValue` conventions.

```
<!-- BaseInput.vue -->
<script setup>
import { defineProps, defineEmits } from 'vue'

const props = defineProps(['modelValue'])
const emit = defineEmits(['update:modelValue'])

const onInput = (e) => {
  emit('update:modelValue', e.target.value)
}
</script>
```

```
<template>
  <input :value="modelValue" @input="onInput" />
</template>
```

Used like this:

```
<script setup>
import { ref } from 'vue'
import BaseInput from './BaseInput.vue'

const username = ref('')
</script>

<template>
  <BaseInput v-model="username" />
</template>
```

This pattern lets you reuse styled or logic-enhanced input fields across your app while maintaining the simplicity of v-model.

Exercise: Basic Contact Form with Confirmation

Let's put together a contact form that:

Collects name, email, and message

Shows a confirmation when submitted

```
<script setup>
import { reactive, ref } from 'vue'

const form = reactive({
  name: '',
  email: '',
  message: ''
})

const submitted = ref(false)

const submit = () => {
  if (!form.name || !form.email || !form.message)
return
  console.log('Form submitted:', { ...form })
  submitted.value = true
```

```
    }
</script>

<template>
  <form @submit.prevent="submit" v-if="!submitted">
    <input v-model="form.name" placeholder="Your
name" />
    <input v-model="form.email" placeholder="Your
email" />
    <textarea v-model="form.message"
placeholder="Message" />

    <button type="submit">Send</button>
  </form>

  <p v-else>Thank you, {{ form.name }}! Your
message has been sent.</p>
</template>
```

This is a fully working contact form:

State is cleanly organized in `form`

Submission is blocked if any field is empty

Confirmation is displayed after submission

Working with forms in Vue is not a complex task once you understand how reactivity, `v-model`, and the DOM work together. Vue's declarative binding style helps you avoid repetitive boilerplate and allows you to focus on the data and user interaction.

Through `ref()` and `reactive()`, you manage form state in a centralized, reactive way. `v-model` keeps the DOM and your state in sync automatically. You can progressively enhance your forms with composables, validation libraries, and reusable input components as your needs grow.

What is Two-Way Binding?

When we talk about two-way binding, we're referring to a process where a value flows **from the component's state to the input element**, and **from the input element back to the component's state** automatically.

162

You can think of it as a continuous feedback loop:

When the model (the state) changes, the input updates.

When the user changes the input, the model updates.

Vue handles this loop behind the scenes using event listeners (`input`, `change`, etc.) and reactive bindings. The `v-model` directive is just syntactic sugar that simplifies the code you would otherwise have to write manually.

How `v-model` Works with Native Inputs

Let's start with a basic example:

```
<script setup>
import { ref } from 'vue'

const name = ref('')
</script>

<template>
  <input v-model="name" placeholder="Enter your name" />
  <p>Hello, {{ name }}</p>
</template>
```

This one line of code:

```
<input v-model="name" />
```

Is functionally equivalent to this more verbose version:

```
<input :value="name" @input="event => name = event.target.value" />
```

That's what `v-model` does for you. It binds the `value` of the input to your state, and it listens for input events to update your state when the user types.

And because `name` is a `ref`, the change is tracked reactively. Any updates to `name.value` will re-render the template anywhere that variable is used.

Controlling Data Flow Between Multiple Fields

You can use `v-model` with multiple fields easily, and they all remain independently reactive.

```
<script setup>
import { ref } from 'vue'

const email = ref('')
const password = ref('')
</script>

<template>
  <form>
    <input v-model="email" type="email"
placeholder="Email" />
    <input v-model="password" type="password"
placeholder="Password" />
    <p>Entered email: {{ email }}</p>
    <p>Entered password: {{ password }}</p>
  </form>
</template>
```

This pattern scales naturally and is very readable. You can use `ref` for single values or group multiple values into a `reactive()` object if you prefer a structured approach.

Working with Selects, Checkboxes, and Radios

The `v-model` directive works on all standard form elements. Vue adapts automatically depending on the type of input.

For example, checkboxes can either be bound to a boolean or an array:

Single checkbox (boolean):

```
<script setup>
import { ref } from 'vue'

const agreed = ref(false)
</script>

<template>
  <input type="checkbox" v-model="agreed" />
  <label>Agree to terms</label>
```

```
</template>
```

Multiple checkboxes (array):

```
<script setup>
import { ref } from 'vue'

const selectedColors = ref([])
</script>

<template>
  <label><input type="checkbox" value="red" v-
model="selectedColors" /> Red</label>
  <label><input type="checkbox" value="green" v-
model="selectedColors" /> Green</label>
  <label><input type="checkbox" value="blue" v-
model="selectedColors" /> Blue</label>

  <p>Selected colors: {{ selectedColors }}</p>
</template>
```

For **radio buttons**, the binding works as a single selected value:

```
<script setup>
import { ref } from 'vue'

const gender = ref('')
</script>

<template>
  <label><input type="radio" value="male" v-
model="gender" /> Male</label>
  <label><input type="radio" value="female" v-
model="gender" /> Female</label>
</template>
```

And for **select dropdowns**, Vue syncs the selected option automatically:

```
<script setup>
import { ref } from 'vue'

const country = ref('')
</script>
```

```
<template>
  <select v-model="country">
    <option value="us">United States</option>
    <option value="uk">United Kingdom</option>
    <option value="ng">Nigeria</option>
  </select>
</template>
```

Vue knows exactly how to map the selected value to the bound variable and will update it when a new option is selected.

Using v-model with Custom Components

One of the most powerful (and often misunderstood) features of v-model is how it works with custom components.

When you use v-model on a custom component, Vue looks for a modelValue prop and expects the component to emit an event called update:modelValue.

Here's how you define a custom input component that supports v-model:

```
<!-- BaseInput.vue -->
<script setup>
const props = defineProps(['modelValue'])
const emit = defineEmits(['update:modelValue'])

const onInput = (e) => {
  emit('update:modelValue', e.target.value)
}
</script>

<template>
  <input :value="modelValue" @input="onInput" />
</template>
```

To use this component:

```
<script setup>
import { ref } from 'vue'
import BaseInput from './BaseInput.vue'

const username = ref('')
</script>
```

```
<template>
  <BaseInput v-model="username" />
  <p>Username: {{ username }}</p>
</template>
```

This setup works the same as native inputs:

The parent passes the value using `v-model`

The child emits `update:modelValue` when its state changes

Vue updates the parent state automatically

Customizing `v-model` Argument and Event

Vue 3 allows you to have **multiple v-model bindings** by customizing the prop and event names. This is helpful when a component needs to expose more than one reactive value.

```
<!-- BaseToggle.vue -->
<script setup>
const props = defineProps({
  modelValue: Boolean,
  label: String
})

const emit = defineEmits(['update:modelValue'])

const toggle = () => {
  emit('update:modelValue', !props.modelValue)
}
</script>

<template>
  <button @click="toggle">
    {{ label }}: {{ modelValue ? 'On' : 'Off' }}
  </button>
</template>
```

Usage:

```
<BaseToggle v-model="isEnabled" label="Dark Mode"
/>
```

167

To use **multiple** `v-models`:

```
<!-- MyComponent.vue -->
<script setup>
const props = defineProps(['titleValue',
'checkedValue'])
const emit = defineEmits(['update:titleValue',
'update:checkedValue'])
</script>

<template>
  <input :value="titleValue" @input="e =>
emit('update:titleValue', e.target.value)" />
  <input type="checkbox" :checked="checkedValue"
@change="e => emit('update:checkedValue',
e.target.checked)" />
</template>
```

Used like this:

```
<MyComponent
  v-model:titleValue="postTitle"
  v-model:checkedValue="isPublished"
/>
```

This kind of setup gives you full flexibility in designing your reusable input and form components.

Exercise: v-model in a Controlled Toggle Component

Here's a quick exercise to reinforce how `v-model` works with a custom toggle switch.

```
<!-- ToggleSwitch.vue -->
<script setup>
const props = defineProps(['modelValue'])
const emit = defineEmits(['update:modelValue'])

const toggle = () => {
  emit('update:modelValue', !props.modelValue)
}
</script>

<template>
```

```
    <div @click="toggle" class="switch" :class="{ on:
modelValue }">
      {{ modelValue ? 'ON' : 'OFF' }}
    </div>
</template>

<style scoped>
.switch {
  width: 100px;
  padding: 10px;
  background: #eee;
  text-align: center;
  cursor: pointer;
}
.switch.on {
  background: #0c0;
  color: white;
}
</style>
```

Used in parent:

```
<script setup>
import { ref } from 'vue'
import ToggleSwitch from './ToggleSwitch.vue'

const lightOn = ref(false)
</script>

<template>
  <ToggleSwitch v-model="lightOn" />
  <p>Light is {{ lightOn ? 'on' : 'off' }}</p>
</template>
```

This shows how v-model works with not only <input> elements but also entirely custom-designed components that emit changes through update:modelValue.

The v-model directive is one of the most developer-friendly features in Vue. It's simple to use, but highly powerful once you understand the mechanics behind it. Whether you're working with native HTML inputs or building custom components, v-model gives you a consistent way to keep user input in sync with your application's reactive state.

169

With it, you avoid verbose event wiring and simplify the feedback loop between the user interface and business logic. In Vue 3, `v-model` goes even further by supporting multiple bindings and fully declarative component design.

Input Validation

Every form is a contract. It's a request from your app to the user: *give me this data so I can do something with it*. But that data needs to be correct, complete, and structured. If it's not, it can break workflows, crash APIs, or cause logical errors downstream.

Validation ensures that:

Users provide what's required

Input matches expected formats

Malicious or accidental misuse is minimized

Your backend or database only receives clean data

When done well, validation also improves usability—by guiding users in real time rather than only blocking them after they submit.

Manual Validation Using Composition API

The simplest and most flexible approach is to write custom validation logic directly in your component using `ref()` or `reactive()` and a bit of conditional checking.

Here's a clean pattern using the Composition API:

```
<script setup>
import { reactive, ref } from 'vue'

const form = reactive({
  name: '',
  email: ''
})

const errors = reactive({
```

```
  name: '',
  email: ''
})

const validate = () => {
  let isValid = true

  if (!form.name.trim()) {
    errors.name = 'Name is required.'
    isValid = false
  } else {
    errors.name = ''
  }

  if (!form.email.includes('@')) {
    errors.email = 'Enter a valid email address.'
    isValid = false
  } else {
    errors.email = ''
  }

  return isValid
}

const submit = () => {
  if (validate()) {
    console.log('Form submitted:', { ...form })
  }
}
</script>

<template>
  <form @submit.prevent="submit">
    <div>
      <input v-model="form.name" placeholder="Name"
/>
      <span v-if="errors.name" class="error">{{
errors.name }}</span>
    </div>

    <div>
```

```
      <input v-model="form.email"
placeholder="Email" />
      <span v-if="errors.email" class="error">{{
errors.email }}</span>
    </div>

    <button type="submit">Submit</button>
  </form>
</template>
```

In this example:

Each field is part of a `reactive` form model

The `errors` object mirrors the form fields

The `validate()` function checks values and sets errors accordingly

On form submission, if validation passes, the form data is logged or processed

This pattern is excellent when you want full control and don't need complex validation rules.

Field-Level Validation with Computed Properties

You can also build validation rules that respond reactively without explicitly calling a validation function. This works best for simple forms with basic rules.

```
<script setup>
import { ref, computed } from 'vue'

const email = ref('')

const emailError = computed(() => {
  if (!email.value) return 'Email is required.'
  if (!email.value.includes('@')) return 'Invalid
email format.'
  return ''
})
</script>

<template>
```

```
  <input v-model="email" placeholder="Email" />
  <span v-if="emailError">{{ emailError }}</span>
</template>
```

As the user types, the error message updates in real time. This can improve UX when used carefully—but avoid bombarding the user with errors before they've had a chance to finish typing.

For this reason, you might combine computed validation with a flag like `hasTouched` or `wasSubmitted` to control when to show feedback.

Validation Composables

If you're validating similar forms across multiple components, it makes sense to extract reusable logic into a composable.

Here's an example of a basic reusable form validator:

```
// composables/useValidator.js
import { reactive } from 'vue'

export function useValidator(form, rules) {
  const errors = reactive({})

  const validate = () => {
    let isValid = true
    for (const key in rules) {
      const value = form[key]
      const rule = rules[key]
      const message = rule(value)
      errors[key] = message
      if (message) isValid = false
    }
    return isValid
  }

  return { errors, validate }
}
```

Used like this:

```
<script setup>
import { reactive } from 'vue'
```

```
import { useValidator } from
'@/composables/useValidator'

const form = reactive({
  username: '',
  password: ''
})

const rules = {
  username: val => !val ? 'Username is required.' :
'',
  password: val => val.length < 6 ? 'Password must
be at least 6 characters.' : ''
}

const { errors, validate } = useValidator(form,
rules)

const submit = () => {
  if (validate()) {
    console.log('Form is valid:', { ...form })
  }
}
</script>

<template>
  <form @submit.prevent="submit">
    <div>
      <input v-model="form.username"
placeholder="Username" />
      <span>{{ errors.username }}</span>
    </div>
    <div>
      <input type="password" v-
model="form.password" placeholder="Password" />
      <span>{{ errors.password }}</span>
    </div>
    <button type="submit">Login</button>
  </form>
</template>
```

This approach lets you reuse the validator with any form by simply changing the rules.

Using HTML5 Built-In Validation

If your form is simple and your users are on modern browsers, you can use the built-in validation features provided by HTML5:

```
<template>
  <form @submit.prevent="submit">
    <input type="email" v-model="email" required />
    <input type="password" v-model="password"
required minlength="6" />
    <button type="submit">Submit</button>
  </form>
</template>
```

You can also trigger built-in browser validation programmatically:

```
const submit = (e) => {
  const formElement = e.target.closest('form')
  if (!formElement.checkValidity()) {
    formElement.reportValidity()
    return
  }

  // Proceed if form is valid
}
```

While this approach is lightweight, it offers less flexibility and customization.

Combining Manual and Library Validation

For more complex validation scenarios—like conditionally required fields, password strength, email confirmation, or form-wide consistency—it's often better to use a validation library.

Libraries like **Vuelidate**, **Yup**, **Zod**, and **vee-validate** allow you to:

Define validation schemas

Validate dynamically or on submission

Show error messages contextually

Integrate easily with Composition API

Each library has its own syntax and strengths. We'll explore their use in depth in the next section, but the key is this: **you can start with manual validation, and scale into a library as your needs grow.**

Input validation isn't just a yes/no check. It's an ongoing conversation between your application and your user:

It guides the user to complete the form correctly

It prevents invalid data from flowing into your system

It increases trust by making your interface predictable and supportive

In Vue 3, the Composition API makes it easier to structure your validation logic clearly—grouped alongside the state it checks, scoped to each form, and reusable wherever needed.

Form Validation with Yup

Yup is a JavaScript validation library that lets you define a schema—essentially a set of validation rules for your form—and then use that schema to validate your data.

Installing Yup

To start using Yup, install it with:

```
npm install yup
```

Creating a Schema-Based Form in Vue 3

Let's say you have a form that collects a user's name, email, and password. You want to ensure that:

The name is required

The email must be valid

The password must be at least 6 characters

Here's how to do that using Vue 3 and the Composition API:

```
<script setup>
import { reactive, ref } from 'vue'
import * as yup from 'yup'

const form = reactive({
  name: '',
  email: '',
  password: ''
})

const errors = reactive({
  name: '',
  email: '',
  password: ''
})

const submitting = ref(false)

const schema = yup.object({
  name: yup.string().required('Name is required.'),
  email: yup.string().email('Email must be
valid.').required('Email is required.'),
  password: yup.string().min(6, 'Password must be
at least 6 characters.').required('Password is
required.')
})

const submit = async () => {
  submitting.value = true
  try {
    await schema.validate(form, { abortEarly: false
})
    Object.keys(errors).forEach(key => errors[key]
= '')
    console.log('Form submitted:', { ...form })
  } catch (validationError) {
    if (validationError.inner) {
      validationError.inner.forEach(err => {
        errors[err.path] = err.message
      })
    }
  } finally {
```

```
      submitting.value = false
   }
}
</script>

<template>
  <form @submit.prevent="submit">
    <div>
      <label>Name</label>
      <input v-model="form.name" />
      <span class="error" v-if="errors.name">{{
errors.name }}</span>
    </div>

    <div>
      <label>Email</label>
      <input v-model="form.email" />
      <span class="error" v-if="errors.email">{{
errors.email }}</span>
    </div>

    <div>
      <label>Password</label>
      <input type="password" v-
model="form.password" />
      <span class="error" v-if="errors.password">{{
errors.password }}</span>
    </div>

    <button type="submit"
:disabled="submitting">Submit</button>
  </form>
</template>

<style scoped>
.error {
  color: red;
  font-size: 0.875rem;
  margin-top: 4px;
  display: block;
}
</style>
```

Why Yup Works Well

You define your rules once in a central schema

You don't have to manually check each field

It supports nested objects, custom rules, and conditional logic

You can reuse the schema on the backend if you're using Node.js with the same validation logic

This approach scales well. If your form grows to 10 or 20 fields, you can still manage everything through the schema, and your logic stays consistent and testable.

Form Validation with Vuelidate

Vuelidate is a Vue-specific validation library that integrates deeply with Vue's reactivity system. Instead of creating a validation schema in a separate object, you define your validation rules right alongside your reactive state.

Installing Vuelidate

You can add it with:

```
npm install @vuelidate/core @vuelidate/validators
```

Using Vuelidate with Composition API

Let's build the same form example, but this time using Vuelidate.

```
<script setup>
import { reactive, ref, computed } from 'vue'
import useVuelidate from '@vuelidate/core'
import { required, email, minLength } from
'@vuelidate/validators'

const form = reactive({
  name: '',
  email: '',
  password: ''
})

const rules = {
```

```
  name: { required },
  email: { required, email },
  password: { required, minLength: minLength(6) }
}

const v$ = useVuelidate(rules, form)
const submitting = ref(false)

const submit = async () => {
  submitting.value = true
  await v$.value.$validate()

  if (v$.value.$error) {
    console.log('Validation failed')
    submitting.value = false
    return
  }

  console.log('Form submitted:', { ...form })
  submitting.value = false
}
</script>

<template>
  <form @submit.prevent="submit">
    <div>
      <label>Name</label>
      <input v-model="form.name" />
      <span class="error" v-if="v$.name.$error &&
v$.name.required.$invalid">Name is required.</span>
    </div>

    <div>
      <label>Email</label>
      <input v-model="form.email" />
      <span class="error" v-if="v$.email.$error">
        <template v-
if="v$.email.required.$invalid">Email is
required.</template>
        <template v-else-
if="v$.email.email.$invalid">Email must be
valid.</template>
```

```
      </span>
    </div>

    <div>
      <label>Password</label>
      <input type="password" v-
model="form.password" />
      <span class="error" v-
if="v$.password.$error">
        <template v-
if="v$.password.required.$invalid">Password is
required.</template>
        <template v-else-
if="v$.password.minLength.$invalid">Password must
be at least 6 characters.</template>
      </span>
    </div>

    <button type="submit"
:disabled="submitting">Submit</button>
  </form>
</template>
```

What Makes Vuelidate a Good Fit

It tracks validation state per field (`$dirty`, `$invalid`, `$pending`)

You can react to validation states in templates without having to manage error messages manually

Validators are composable and can be reused

Great for reactive and dynamic forms with changing rules

Unlike Yup, which separates validation schema from data, Vuelidate binds them together. This is sometimes more convenient, especially in smaller or medium-sized applications.

Choosing Between Yup and Vuelidate

Both libraries are excellent, but they serve slightly different use cases.

Use **Yup** when:

You prefer schema-based validation

You already use it with your backend or Node.js stack

You want to extract validation into standalone reusable schemas or composables

You are already using `reactive()` for form data and want a decoupled approach

Use **Vuelidate** when:

You want validation rules to live directly alongside your component logic

You want deeper template integration with features like `$dirty` or `$pending`

Your form state is deeply nested or needs conditional validation on the fly

You prefer validation to live closer to the reactivity system and template

There's no wrong choice—it depends on the architecture of your app and how much abstraction you want.

Handling validation manually is fine for simple forms. But as your forms grow in complexity, you need strategies and tools that scale with you. Libraries like **Yup** and **Vuelidate** give you flexibility, clarity, and maintainability.

Yup lets you extract and centralize rules as schemas. Vuelidate lets you define reactive rules that live directly with your component logic. You can even use both in the same application if the context demands it.

Why Use Composition API for Forms

A form isn't just inputs and buttons. It involves multiple behaviors working together:

Keeping track of input state

Performing validation

Controlling loading or submission states

Resetting form data

Conditionally showing feedback or error messages

In the Options API, this logic is often split between `data()`, `methods`, `computed`, and lifecycle hooks. That fragmentation makes it harder to understand, test, and reuse.

With the Composition API, you bring it all together. You define your reactive state and all the behavior related to that state in the same block or function. That makes your forms easier to reason about, and gives you the ability to extract and reuse logic as needed.

Reactive Form State with `reactive()`

The most natural way to represent a form using the Composition API is with a single reactive object:

```
<script setup>
import { reactive } from 'vue'

const form = reactive({
  name: '',
  email: '',
  message: ''
})

const submit = () => {
  console.log('Form submitted:', { ...form })
}
</script>

<template>
  <form @submit.prevent="submit">
    <input v-model="form.name" placeholder="Your name" />
    <input v-model="form.email" placeholder="Your email" />
    <textarea v-model="form.message" placeholder="Your message"></textarea>
    <button type="submit">Send</button>
  </form>
</template>
```

All state is grouped together inside `form`, which makes it easy to manage, reset, or pass around. Vue tracks changes to each property and automatically updates the template when those values change.

Adding Validation Logic

You can define your own validation rules directly in the same `setup()` block. Here's an example using manual validation:

```
<script setup>
import { reactive, ref } from 'vue'

const form = reactive({
  name: '',
  email: '',
  message: ''
})

const errors = reactive({
  name: '',
  email: '',
  message: ''
})

const validate = () => {
  let isValid = true

  if (!form.name.trim()) {
    errors.name = 'Name is required.'
    isValid = false
  } else {
    errors.name = ''
  }

  if (!form.email.includes('@')) {
    errors.email = 'Enter a valid email address.'
    isValid = false
  } else {
    errors.email = ''
  }

  if (!form.message.trim()) {
```

```
      errors.message = 'Message cannot be empty.'
      isValid = false
    } else {
      errors.message = ''
    }

    return isValid
}

const submit = () => {
  if (!validate()) return
  console.log('Form is valid. Submitting:', {
...form })
}
</script>

<template>
  <form @submit.prevent="submit">
    <div>
      <input v-model="form.name" placeholder="Name"
/>
      <span v-if="errors.name" class="error">{{
errors.name }}</span>
    </div>

    <div>
      <input v-model="form.email"
placeholder="Email" />
      <span v-if="errors.email" class="error">{{
errors.email }}</span>
    </div>

    <div>
      <textarea v-model="form.message"
placeholder="Message"></textarea>
      <span v-if="errors.message" class="error">{{
errors.message }}</span>
    </div>

    <button type="submit">Submit</button>
  </form>
</template>
```

```
<style scoped>
.error {
  color: red;
  font-size: 0.9em;
}
</style>
```

This pattern keeps your form state and validation logic bundled together, which improves maintainability and keeps each component self-contained.

Adding Submit State and Reset Logic

When building production-ready forms, you often need to:

Disable the form during submission

Show loading indicators

Reset the form after a successful submit

You can add this logic easily using `ref()`:

```
<script setup>
import { reactive, ref } from 'vue'

const form = reactive({
  email: '',
  password: ''
})

const errors = reactive({
  email: '',
  password: ''
})

const submitting = ref(false)
const submitted = ref(false)

const validate = () => {
  let valid = true

  errors.email = form.email.includes('@') ? '' :
'Email is invalid.'
```

186

```
  errors.password = form.password.length >= 6 ? ''
: 'Password must be at least 6 characters.'

  if (errors.email || errors.password) valid =
false

  return valid
}

const resetForm = () => {
  form.email = ''
  form.password = ''
  submitted.value = false
}

const submit = async () => {
  submitted.value = false
  if (!validate()) return

  submitting.value = true

  await new Promise(resolve => setTimeout(resolve,
1000)) // simulate async operation

  submitted.value = true
  submitting.value = false
}
</script>

<template>
  <form @submit.prevent="submit">
    <input v-model="form.email" placeholder="Email"
/>
    <span class="error" v-if="errors.email">{{
errors.email }}</span>

    <input type="password" v-model="form.password"
placeholder="Password" />
    <span class="error" v-if="errors.password">{{
errors.password }}</span>
```

```
    <button type="submit"
:disabled="submitting">Login</button>
    <button type="button"
@click="resetForm">Reset</button>

    <p v-if="submitted">Form submitted
successfully!</p>
  </form>
</template>
```

This version adds features often requested by users: disabling the submit button, resetting the form, and showing a submission result.

Extracting Form Logic into a Composable

When your app has multiple forms, it makes sense to extract common patterns into reusable logic. With Composition API, that's easy to do using a composable.

Here's an example:

```
// composables/useContactForm.js
import { reactive, ref } from 'vue'

export function useContactForm() {
  const form = reactive({
    name: '',
    email: '',
    message: ''
  })

  const errors = reactive({
    name: '',
    email: '',
    message: ''
  })

  const submitting = ref(false)
  const submitted = ref(false)

  const validate = () => {
    let valid = true
```

```
    errors.name = form.name ? '' : 'Name is
required.'
    errors.email = form.email.includes('@') ? '' :
'Email is invalid.'
    errors.message = form.message ? '' : 'Message
is required.'

    if (errors.name || errors.email ||
errors.message) valid = false

    return valid
  }

  const submit = async () => {
    if (!validate()) return
    submitting.value = true
    await new Promise(resolve =>
setTimeout(resolve, 1000))
    submitted.value = true
    submitting.value = false
  }

  return {
    form,
    errors,
    submitting,
    submitted,
    submit
  }
}
```

Then use it like this in your component:

```
<script setup>
import { useContactForm } from
'@/composables/useContactForm'

const { form, errors, submitting, submitted, submit
} = useContactForm()
</script>

<template>
  <form @submit.prevent="submit">
```

```
    <input v-model="form.name" placeholder="Name"
/>
    <span v-if="errors.name">{{ errors.name
}}</span>

    <input v-model="form.email" placeholder="Email"
/>
    <span v-if="errors.email">{{ errors.email
}}</span>

    <textarea v-model="form.message"
placeholder="Message"></textarea>
    <span v-if="errors.message">{{ errors.message
}}</span>

    <button :disabled="submitting">Send</button>

    <p v-if="submitted">Thanks for contacting
us!</p>
  </form>
</template>
```

This approach lets you isolate form behavior and logic, test it independently, and reuse it across different pages or layouts.

The Composition API gives you a clear, organized way to structure form logic. It allows:

Grouping of state, validation, and actions in one place

Easy refactoring of logic into composables

Scalability as your form requirements grow

Full control over user experience (submission state, validation feedback, etc.)

Whether you're building a contact form, login form, or complex multi-step wizard, Composition API keeps your code modular and consistent. Forms become easier to write, debug, and extend because everything related to the form lives in one logical unit.

Chapter 7: Managing Application State with Vuex

When you start working with larger projects, you'll often run into a very common question: *How do I manage state across components efficiently?* That's exactly the problem Vuex is designed to solve. In this chapter, we'll explore Vuex in depth: what it is, why it's useful, how its core concepts work, how to modularize a store, how to use it with the Composition API, and finally, how to structure state management for real application features like authentication, carts, and UI behavior.

What is Vuex ?

When you first start developing with Vue, managing state usually feels straightforward. You define your data inside a component's `setup()` or `data()` function, you bind it to inputs with `v-model`, and you pass it around through props or emit events when you need to communicate between components. For smaller applications, or for isolated pieces of UI, this approach works well.

But applications don't stay small for long. As features grow, and more components are added, you'll begin to notice some friction. You might find yourself passing props three levels deep just to display a value in a nested component. You might need two sibling components to react to the same piece of data. You might want to share data like user authentication status, shopping cart items, or UI state like "sidebar open/closed" across many views.

That's where Vuex steps in. Vuex is a **centralized state management system** built specifically for Vue. It provides a structured way to store, update, and retrieve shared application data from a **single source of truth**.

Instead of scattering state across components, Vuex keeps it all in one store. Every component can access it, update it through controlled methods, and respond reactively to changes. You get predictable state flow, clearer debugging, and scalable architecture.

Let's go deeper into how Vuex changes the way you manage state and what that looks like in practice.

The Problem Vuex Solves

Here's a scenario many developers run into:

You're building an e-commerce site. You have:

A `Header` component that shows how many items are in the cart.

A `ProductList` component that adds items to the cart.

A `CartDrawer` component that shows the contents of the cart.

Each of these components needs access to the same cart data. Without Vuex, you might try to manage this by:

Passing the cart as a prop from a parent component

Emitting events upward when something changes

Using a global event bus or an injected object

But these solutions are brittle. Props and emits require tightly-coupled hierarchies. Global event buses become difficult to track and debug. Eventually, you lose control over **when and how** state is changed.

Vuex solves this by giving you a **global store**—a reactive object that any component can read from and write to, but only through well-defined actions.

Understanding Centralized State

The central idea behind Vuex is that you define **one central place** where your application's state lives. This store contains:

The raw data (`state`)

Functions that modify the data (`mutations`)

Logic that may include asynchronous calls (`actions`)

Derivative values (`getters`)

You never modify the state directly from your components. Instead, you call actions, which commit mutations. This strict flow means all data changes go through a consistent pipeline.

This design eliminates surprises. You always know *what* caused a change in the state, *when* it happened, and *where* it was triggered. That's a big deal for debugging and scaling.

A Real Working Example

Let's walk through a working Vuex setup in a Vue 3 app that manages user login state.

1. Install Vuex (if you haven't yet):

```
npm install vuex@next
```

2. Create the store:

```
// store/index.js
import { createStore } from 'vuex'

const store = createStore({
  state: () => ({
    user: null
  }),

  mutations: {
    SET_USER(state, payload) {
      state.user = payload
    },
    LOGOUT(state) {
      state.user = null
    }
  },

  actions: {
    login({ commit }, credentials) {
      // simulate an async login
      setTimeout(() => {
        commit('SET_USER', {
          name: credentials.username,
          token: 'abc123'
```

```
      })
    }, 1000)
  },

  logout({ commit }) {
    commit('LOGOUT')
  }
},

getters: {
  isAuthenticated(state) {
    return !!state.user
  },
  username(state) {
    return state.user?.name || 'Guest'
  }
}
})

export default store
```

3. Use the store in your main application:

```
// main.js
import { createApp } from 'vue'
import App from './App.vue'
import store from './store'

createApp(App).use(store).mount('#app')
```

4. Access it in a component:

```
<!-- components/UserPanel.vue -->
<script setup>
import { useStore } from 'vuex'
import { computed } from 'vue'

const store = useStore()

const username = computed(() =>
store.getters.username)
const isLoggedIn = computed(() =>
store.getters.isAuthenticated)
```

```
const login = () => {
  store.dispatch('login', { username: 'Alice' })
}

const logout = () => {
  store.dispatch('logout')
}
</script>

<template>
  <div>
    <p>Welcome, {{ username }}</p>
    <button @click="login" v-
if="!isLoggedIn">Login</button>
    <button @click="logout" v-else>Logout</button>
  </div>
</template>
```

This simple example shows how:

You store your user state centrally.

You never mutate it directly—only through defined actions.

Your components are reactive and clean, with no event emissions or deep prop passing.

Debugging and DevTools

One of the reasons developers love Vuex is how well it integrates with Vue DevTools. Every time you commit a mutation, it shows up in the dev panel. You can inspect:

What the previous state was

What mutation occurred

What the new state looks like

The full history of all changes

You can even time-travel between mutation states.

This makes Vuex not just a code convenience, but also a serious developer productivity tool—especially in larger teams where shared state can be a source of bugs.

When You Don't Need Vuex

It's important to know that Vuex is powerful, but it isn't always necessary.

If your app is small, or most of your state is local to a component or passed only one or two levels deep, the Composition API might be enough. You can even use `provide/inject` or shared composables to simulate centralized state.

But when:

Your app spans many views

Multiple components need shared access to the same data

You need tight control and traceability over state updates

You want DevTools support to debug and inspect state changes

That's when Vuex shines.

Vuex brings structure and discipline to state management in Vue applications. It helps reduce complexity as your project grows, keeps your logic clean and testable, and creates a single, reliable source of truth your entire application can depend on.

---

core concepts of Vuex

The building blocks that make state management with Vuex both structured and powerful. These concepts are: **state**, **getters**, **mutations**, and **actions**. Each of these plays a distinct role in how data flows through a Vue application.

To understand them well, you need to see how they fit together. The goal is to keep application state predictable, centralized, and maintainable. We'll break each one down, build realistic examples, and show how they interact inside a typical Vue 3 application using the Composition API.

State: The Source of Truth

When you use Vuex, your shared data lives in a centralized object called the **state**. It holds the values that need to be accessed by multiple components.

Instead of storing this data in local component state (`ref` or `reactive`), you define it in the Vuex store so it can be shared across the application.

Here's a simple example of Vuex state:

```
// store/index.js
import { createStore } from 'vuex'

const store = createStore({
  state: () => ({
    user: null,
    cartItems: []
  })
})

export default store
```

In this case:

`user` represents the currently logged-in user.

`cartItems` is an array of products the user has added to their cart.

This state is now globally available to any component that imports and uses the store.

Accessing state in a component (with Composition API) looks like this:

```
<script setup>
import { useStore } from 'vuex'
import { computed } from 'vue'

const store = useStore()
const user = computed(() => store.state.user)
const cartItems = computed(() =>
store.state.cartItems)
</script>
```

The use of `computed()` ensures your component updates reactively whenever the state changes.

Getters: Computed Properties for Your Store

Getters allow you to define **derived state** based on your actual state. These are similar to computed properties in components. They are useful when:

You want to encapsulate logic to calculate a value based on state

You need to reuse that logic in multiple places

You want to cache results reactively

Let's define some getters:

```js
// store/index.js
const store = createStore({
  state: () => ({
    user: null,
    cartItems: [
      { id: 1, name: 'Shoes', price: 50 },
      { id: 2, name: 'Hat', price: 20 }
    ]
  }),

  getters: {
    isAuthenticated(state) {
      return !!state.user
    },

    cartTotalPrice(state) {
      return state.cartItems.reduce((total, item)
=> total + item.price, 0)
    }
  }
})
```

Usage in a component:

```js
<script setup>
import { useStore } from 'vuex'
import { computed } from 'vue'
```

```
const store = useStore()

const isAuthenticated = computed(() =>
store.getters.isAuthenticated)
const cartTotal = computed(() =>
store.getters.cartTotalPrice)
</script>
```

Using getters helps you **keep logic out of the component** and **centralize it in the store**, which is especially helpful when multiple components rely on the same derived value.

Mutations: The Only Way to Change State

In Vuex, you are not allowed to directly mutate the state from your component. Instead, Vuex enforces a strict pattern: **you must use mutations**.

Mutations are synchronous functions that directly modify state. Each mutation takes two arguments:

The current state

A payload (any data you want to pass in)

Example:

```
mutations: {
  SET_USER(state, user) {
    state.user = user
  },
  ADD_TO_CART(state, item) {
    state.cartItems.push(item)
  },
  REMOVE_FROM_CART(state, itemId) {
    state.cartItems = state.cartItems.filter(item
=> item.id !== itemId)
  }
}
```

To call a mutation, use `store.commit()`:

```
<script setup>
import { useStore } from 'vuex'

const store = useStore()
```

199

```
const login = () => {
  const userData = { name: 'Alex', id: 1 }
  store.commit('SET_USER', userData)
}

const removeItem = (id) => {
  store.commit('REMOVE_FROM_CART', id)
}
</script>
```

Mutations should be simple and focused—they **do one thing** to the state. No asynchronous logic should go in mutations. This makes them highly predictable and traceable.

Actions: Business Logic and Async Operations

If mutations are the only way to change state, **actions** are the only place you should perform **asynchronous logic**.

Actions handle things like:

Fetching data from an API

Performing authentication

Submitting forms to a server

Once the async operation is complete, the action commits one or more mutations.

Here's an example of an action that fetches user data from an API:

```
actions: {

  async login({ commit }, credentials) {
    try {
      const response = await
fakeLoginAPI(credentials)
      commit('SET_USER', response.data)
    } catch (error) {
      console.error('Login failed:', error)
    }
  },
```

```
  async fetchCart({ commit }) {
    const response = await fetch('/api/cart')
    const data = await response.json()
    data.forEach(item => commit('ADD_TO_CART',
item))
  }
}
```

Calling an action from your component is done via `store.dispatch()`:

```
<script setup>
import { useStore } from 'vuex'

const store = useStore()

const handleLogin = () => {
  store.dispatch('login', { username: 'alex',
password: 'secret' })
}
</script>
```

By using actions:

You keep asynchronous logic out of your components

You maintain a clean separation between **logic** and **state updates**

You ensure that all state changes still go through mutations, preserving trackability

Putting It All Together: A Practical Example

Let's walk through a complete example for managing user authentication:

1. Vuex Store

```
// store/index.js
import { createStore } from 'vuex'

const store = createStore({
  state: () => ({
    user: null
  }),
```

```
  getters: {
    isLoggedIn(state) {
      return !!state.user
    },
    username(state) {
      return state.user?.name || 'Guest'
    }
  },

  mutations: {
    SET_USER(state, user) {
      state.user = user
    },
    LOGOUT(state) {
      state.user = null
    }
  },

  actions: {
    async login({ commit }, credentials) {
      // fake API simulation
      await new Promise(resolve =>
setTimeout(resolve, 1000))
      const user = { name: credentials.username }
      commit('SET_USER', user)
    },

    logout({ commit }) {
      commit('LOGOUT')
    }
  }
})

export default store
```

2. Using in a Component

```
<script setup>
import { useStore } from 'vuex'
import { computed } from 'vue'

const store = useStore()
```

```
const username = computed(() =>
store.getters.username)
const isLoggedIn = computed(() =>
store.getters.isLoggedIn)

const login = () => {
  store.dispatch('login', { username: 'Alice' })
}

const logout = () => {
  store.dispatch('logout')
}
</script>

<template>
  <div>
    <p>Welcome, {{ username }}</p>
    <button v-if="!isLoggedIn"
@click="login">Login</button>
    <button v-else @click="logout">Logout</button>
  </div>
</template>
```

This is a complete setup that:

Stores login data centrally in Vuex

Lets any component access or react to login status

Separates view logic (buttons and UI) from state logic (store)

Vuex is built around a few key principles:

Centralized state makes it easier to share and manage application data

Predictable mutations help you track and debug every change

Asynchronous logic belongs in actions, not in your components

Getters keep computed logic out of your templates and inside the store

When used properly, these core concepts make it much easier to develop and scale Vue applications—especially those with complex state, shared logic, and many components needing access to the same data.

Modularizing the Vuex Store

As your application grows, your Vuex store can start to become a dumping ground for unrelated state, actions, mutations, and getters. You might begin with just a few properties like `user` and `cart`, but over time, you find yourself tracking things like settings, products, orders, filters, pagination, notifications, loading states, and more.

If all of that logic lives inside a single store definition, the file becomes difficult to maintain. You lose separation of concerns. You also risk accidentally introducing bugs, since it's easier to make conflicting updates when everything is tightly packed into one place.

To solve this, Vuex supports **modules**. A module is a self-contained piece of your store that manages its own state, mutations, actions, and getters. Think of each module as a mini store that is namespaced and composable.

Modularization helps you:

Organize related logic into its own space

Reuse structure across features

Make your application easier to reason about

Improve testability and maintainability

Starting with a Flat Store

Let's say your app has two major pieces of state:

Authentication

Shopping cart

In a flat Vuex store, you might have everything declared together:

```
// store/index.js (non-modular)
```

204

```
import { createStore } from 'vuex'

const store = createStore({
  state: () => ({
    user: null,
    token: null,
    cartItems: []
  }),

  mutations: {
    SET_USER(state, payload) {
      state.user = payload.user
      state.token = payload.token
    },
    LOGOUT(state) {
      state.user = null
      state.token = null
    },
    ADD_TO_CART(state, item) {
      state.cartItems.push(item)
    },
    REMOVE_FROM_CART(state, id) {
      state.cartItems = state.cartItems.filter(i =>
i.id !== id)
    }
  },

  actions: {
    login({ commit }, credentials) {
      commit('SET_USER', {
        user: { name: credentials.username },
        token: 'abc123'
      })
    },
    logout({ commit }) {
      commit('LOGOUT')
    },
    addToCart({ commit }, item) {
      commit('ADD_TO_CART', item)
    }
  }
})
```

```
export default store
```
This works, but as the app scales, this store will become harder to manage. It lacks structure, and there's no separation between authentication and cart logic.

Creating Vuex Modules

The better approach is to **split your store into logical modules,** with each module having its own scope and responsibility.

Let's create two separate modules: `auth` and `cart`.

auth.js

```
// store/modules/auth.js
export default {
  namespaced: true,

  state: () => ({
    user: null,
    token: null
  }),

  mutations: {
    SET_USER(state, payload) {
      state.user = payload.user
      state.token = payload.token
    },
    LOGOUT(state) {
      state.user = null
      state.token = null
    }
  },

  actions: {
    login({ commit }, credentials) {
      // simulate login
      const payload = {
        user: { name: credentials.username },
        token: 'xyz123'
      }
      commit('SET_USER', payload)
```

206

```
    },
    logout({ commit }) {
      commit('LOGOUT')
    }
  },

  getters: {
    isLoggedIn: (state) => !!state.user,
    username: (state) => state.user?.name ||
'Guest'
  }
}
```

cart.js

```
// store/modules/cart.js
export default {
  namespaced: true,

  state: () => ({
    items: []
  }),

  mutations: {
    ADD_ITEM(state, item) {
      state.items.push(item)
    },
    REMOVE_ITEM(state, id) {
      state.items = state.items.filter(i => i.id
!== id)
    },
    CLEAR_CART(state) {
      state.items = []
    }
  },

  actions: {
    addItem({ commit }, item) {
      commit('ADD_ITEM', item)
    },
    removeItem({ commit }, id) {
      commit('REMOVE_ITEM', id)
    },
```

```
    clearCart({ commit }) {
      commit('CLEAR_CART')
    }
  },

  getters: {
    itemCount: (state) => state.items.length,
    totalAmount: (state) =>
state.items.reduce((sum, item) => sum + item.price,
0)
  }
}
```

Now each module is focused, testable, and organized.

Registering Modules in the Store

With these modules in place, your main store becomes much cleaner:

```
// store/index.js
import { createStore } from 'vuex'
import auth from './modules/auth'
import cart from './modules/cart'

const store = createStore({
  modules: {
    auth,
    cart
  }
})

export default store
```

Each module is registered under a key that becomes its **namespace** (in this case, auth and cart). All its state and methods live under that namespace.

Accessing Module State, Getters, Actions, and Mutations

When using Vuex modules, you access each property using its namespace.

In your components:

```
<script setup>
```

```
import { useStore } from 'vuex'
import { computed } from 'vue'

const store = useStore()

const username = computed(() =>
store.getters['auth/username'])
const isLoggedIn = computed(() =>
store.getters['auth/isLoggedIn'])

const cartCount = computed(() =>
store.getters['cart/itemCount'])
const cartTotal = computed(() =>
store.getters['cart/totalAmount'])

const login = () => {
  store.dispatch('auth/login', { username: 'Jane'
})
}

const addToCart = () => {
  const item = { id: 101, name: 'T-shirt', price:
25 }
  store.dispatch('cart/addItem', item)
}
</script>
```

You can see that using `namespace/actionName` or `namespace/getterName` is all you need. Vuex handles the rest internally.

Namespacing

By default, modules are namespaced when `namespaced: true` is set. This:

Prevents naming collisions across modules

Makes it clear where logic belongs

Encourages better design and separation

If you don't namespace modules, all getters, mutations, and actions are registered in the global namespace—which leads to confusion and bugs in larger applications.

Stick to namespacing unless you have a very good reason not to.

Real-World Benefit: Codebase Scalability

Let's say your app has:

Authentication (`auth`)

Shopping cart (`cart`)

Product listing (`products`)

App-wide UI state (`ui`)

Notifications (`notifications`)

Instead of cramming all of that into a single store, you structure it like this:

```
store/
|
├── index.js
└── modules/
    ├── auth.js
    ├── cart.js
    ├── products.js
    ├── ui.js
    └── notifications.js
```

Each module can grow independently. It can be tested in isolation. It can even be dynamically registered later if needed (e.g., feature modules loaded on demand).

Optional: Dynamic Module Registration

Vuex also supports **registering modules dynamically** at runtime. This is useful when working with code-splitting or lazy-loaded routes.

```
store.registerModule('checkout', checkoutModule)
```

You can remove it later:

```
store.unregisterModule('checkout')
```

This gives you even more control over performance and organization in large apps.

Modularization is essential for any medium or large Vuex store. It allows you to:

Separate concerns

Maintain cleaner, testable files

Avoid collisions and coupling

Scale confidently as your app grows

Each Vuex module becomes a unit of logic focused on a specific feature of your app. This structure keeps your store flexible, composable, and readable—even as you add more functionality.

Vuex and Composition API Integration

With the Composition API, Vue gives you more flexibility in how you define logic inside your components. Instead of defining everything inside `data()`, `methods`, and `computed`, you use plain JavaScript functions like `ref()`, `reactive()`, and `computed()` inside the `setup()` function. This change in component design impacts how you interact with Vuex, especially since the legacy syntax like `mapState` and `mapGetters` doesn't fit naturally inside `setup()`.

Vuex supports this fully through the `useStore()` helper. This lets you access the store instance directly and use any part of it within your Composition API logic. You can read state, dispatch actions, commit mutations, or use getters—everything you would normally do in an Options API component, but in a way that works naturally inside `setup()`.

Accessing the Vuex Store with useStore()

To use Vuex inside a component built with the Composition API, you import and call `useStore()` from `vuex`. This returns the store instance, and from there, you can access everything you've defined in your store.

```
<script setup>
import { useStore } from 'vuex'
import { computed } from 'vue'

const store = useStore()

const username = computed(() =>
store.state.auth.user?.name || 'Guest')
const isLoggedIn = computed(() =>
store.getters['auth/isLoggedIn'])

const login = () => {
  store.dispatch('auth/login', { username: 'Alex'
})
}

const logout = () => {
  store.dispatch('auth/logout')
}
</script>

<template>
  <div>
    <p>Welcome, {{ username }}</p>
    <button v-if="!isLoggedIn"
@click="login">Login</button>
    <button v-else @click="logout">Logout</button>
  </div>
</template>
```

In this example:

`useStore()` gives you access to the full Vuex store

`computed()` makes sure you stay reactive when using state and getters

`dispatch()` is used to trigger actions from the store

No prop drilling, no emits—just clean state access

You are writing clear, modern Vue 3 code that works naturally with Vuex.

Why Computed Is Essential

If you were to directly read from `store.state.user`, it would not be reactive. You'd only get a static snapshot of the value at that time. Vue's reactivity system needs to be aware of the dependency so it can re-run when state changes.

To make this work correctly, always wrap state or getters inside `computed()` when using them in templates:

```
const cartTotal = computed(() =>
store.getters['cart/totalPrice'])
```

This ensures that your component reacts to changes automatically.

Committing Mutations from Composition API

When you want to update state using a mutation (synchronous update), you call `store.commit()`:

```
store.commit('cart/ADD_ITEM', { id: 3, name:
'Notebook', price: 8 })
```

This is typically done for straightforward updates like adding or removing items, toggling flags, or setting raw values.

A real example might look like this:

```
<script setup>
import { useStore } from 'vuex'

const store = useStore()

const addItem = () => {
  const product = { id: 5, name: 'Pen', price: 2 }
  store.commit('cart/ADD_ITEM', product)
}
</script>

<template>
```

```
    <button @click="addItem">Add to Cart</button>
</template>
```

This structure keeps mutations simple and ensures state changes are trackable in DevTools.

Dispatching Actions Asynchronously

For asynchronous operations—like calling an API or submitting a form—you should dispatch an action instead of committing directly.

```
const store = useStore()

const submitOrder = () => {
  store.dispatch('cart/submitOrder', { items:
store.state.cart.items })
}
```

Inside the `cart` module:

```
actions: {
  async submitOrder({ commit }, payload) {
    try {
      const response = await fetch('/api/orders', {
        method: 'POST',
        body: JSON.stringify(payload.items)
      })

      const data = await response.json()

      if (data.success) {
        commit('CLEAR_CART')
      }
    } catch (err) {
      console.error('Order submission failed:',
err)
    }
  }
}
```

This structure separates **business logic** (fetching and validating) from **state logic** (mutating the cart), keeping your code easier to reason about and test.

Creating Your Own Composables that Use Vuex

214

One of the biggest strengths of the Composition API is that you can extract common logic into reusable composables.

Let's say you want to abstract the authentication logic into a composable called useAuth().

```js
// composables/useAuth.js
import { useStore } from 'vuex'
import { computed } from 'vue'

export function useAuth() {
  const store = useStore()

  const user = computed(() =>
store.state.auth.user)
  const isLoggedIn = computed(() =>
store.getters['auth/isLoggedIn'])

  const login = (credentials) => {
    store.dispatch('auth/login', credentials)
  }

  const logout = () => {
    store.dispatch('auth/logout')
  }

  return {
    user,
    isLoggedIn,
    login,
    logout
  }
}
```

Now in any component, you can use this like so:

```vue
<script setup>
import { useAuth } from '@/composables/useAuth'

const { user, isLoggedIn, login, logout } =
useAuth()
</script>
```

```
<template>
  <div>
    <p>Hello, {{ user?.name || 'Guest' }}</p>
    <button v-if="!isLoggedIn" @click="login({
username: 'Ali' })">Login</button>
    <button v-else @click="logout">Logout</button>
  </div>
</template>
```

This keeps your components thin and focused on rendering logic, while the business logic lives in well-scoped reusable functions.

Working with Namespaced Modules in Composition API

If you're using Vuex modules that are namespaced (and you should), your access patterns just need to include the namespace:

store.state.auth.user

store.getters['auth/isLoggedIn']

store.commit('auth/SET_USER', user)

store.dispatch('auth/login', credentials)

This structure ensures no overlap in naming between modules, and gives you clean separation of logic—essential in larger applications.

Vue DevTools fully supports the Composition API and Vuex. You can:

Track every mutation and action

Inspect the state tree

Time-travel between state changes

Just ensure you install Vue DevTools and run your app in development mode. Even when using `setup()`, all your store activity remains traceable and visible.

Integrating Vuex with the Composition API is seamless and powerful when done right. Here's what you've seen:

Use `useStore()` to access the Vuex store inside `setup()`

216

Wrap state and getters in `computed()` to keep them reactive

Use `commit()` for synchronous updates, and `dispatch()` for async actions

Build composables around Vuex logic to promote reuse and testability

Always access namespaced modules with full paths like `'cart/addItem'`

By combining Vuex with the Composition API, you get the best of both worlds: a structured, predictable state management system and flexible, reusable logic in your components.

Managing Auth, Cart, and UI State with Vuex

One of the most common, real-world use cases in Vue applications. These types of state are foundational in web apps, particularly those involving user interaction, e-commerce, and interface customization.

Each of these—**authentication**, **shopping cart**, and **UI state**—has its own structure, behavior, and lifecycle. Yet all benefit from being handled via Vuex because they are global, shared concerns that multiple components need to access or react to.

Managing Authentication State

Authentication state refers to whether a user is logged in, who they are, and what permissions or access tokens they may have.

Let's define a Vuex module to handle this:

```
// store/modules/auth.js
export default {
  namespaced: true,

  state: () => ({
    user: null,
    token: null
  }),

  getters: {
```

```
    isLoggedIn(state) {
      return !!state.token
    },
    username(state) {
      return state.user?.name || 'Guest'
    }
  },

  mutations: {
    SET_USER(state, { user, token }) {
      state.user = user
      state.token = token
    },
    LOGOUT(state) {
      state.user = null
      state.token = null
    }
  },

  actions: {
    async login({ commit }, credentials) {
      // Simulate API call
      await new Promise(resolve =>
setTimeout(resolve, 1000))
      const token = 'mock-token-123'
      const user = { id: 1, name:
credentials.username }
      commit('SET_USER', { user, token })
    },

    logout({ commit }) {
      commit('LOGOUT')
    }
  }
}
```

Now register this module in your store:

```
// store/index.js
import { createStore } from 'vuex'
import auth from './modules/auth'

export default createStore({
```

```
  modules: {
    auth
  }
})
```

In a component using the Composition API:

```
<script setup>
import { useStore } from 'vuex'
import { computed } from 'vue'

const store = useStore()

const isLoggedIn = computed(() =>
store.getters['auth/isLoggedIn'])
const username = computed(() =>
store.getters['auth/username'])

const login = () => {
  store.dispatch('auth/login', { username: 'Alice'
})
}

const logout = () => {
  store.dispatch('auth/logout')
}
</script>

<template>
  <div>
    <p>Hello, {{ username }}</p>
    <button v-if="!isLoggedIn"
@click="login">Login</button>
    <button v-else @click="logout">Logout</button>
  </div>
</template>
```

This pattern allows any component to react to login state changes without duplicating logic or relying on props or events.

Managing Shopping Cart State

Cart state is common in e-commerce apps. It typically includes:

A list of products in the cart

Item quantities

Subtotals and totals

Here's how you can structure it in Vuex:

```javascript
// store/modules/cart.js
export default {
  namespaced: true,

  state: () => ({
    items: []
  }),

  getters: {
    itemCount(state) {
      return state.items.length
    },
    totalAmount(state) {
      return state.items.reduce((sum, item) => sum
+ item.price * item.quantity, 0)
    }
  },

  mutations: {
    ADD_ITEM(state, item) {
      const existing = state.items.find(i => i.id
=== item.id)
      if (existing) {
        existing.quantity += item.quantity
      } else {
        state.items.push({ ...item, quantity:
item.quantity || 1 })
      }
    },

    REMOVE_ITEM(state, id) {
      state.items = state.items.filter(item =>
item.id !== id)
    },
```

```
    CLEAR_CART(state) {
      state.items = []
    }
  },

  actions: {
    addItem({ commit }, item) {
      commit('ADD_ITEM', item)
    },
    removeItem({ commit }, id) {
      commit('REMOVE_ITEM', id)
    },
    clearCart({ commit }) {
      commit('CLEAR_CART')
    }
  }
}
```

Register it in your store:

```
import cart from './modules/cart'

export default createStore({
  modules: {
    cart
  }
})
```

Using this in a product component:

```
<script setup>
import { useStore } from 'vuex'
import { computed } from 'vue'

const store = useStore()

const cartItemCount = computed(() =>
store.getters['cart/itemCount'])
const total = computed(() =>
store.getters['cart/totalAmount'])

const addToCart = () => {
```

```
  const product = { id: 7, name: 'Mouse', price:
29.99, quantity: 1 }
  store.dispatch('cart/addItem', product)
}
</script>

<template>
  <div>
    <button @click="addToCart">Add to Cart</button>
    <p>Items in Cart: {{ cartItemCount }}</p>
    <p>Total: ${{ total.toFixed(2) }}</p>
  </div>
</template>
```

Here, the state stays entirely centralized. The logic to calculate totals is handled in getters, and the mutation logic handles merging duplicate items. This is a clean, scalable solution that avoids duplication across components.

Managing UI State

UI state includes things like:

Sidebar visibility

Theme preference

Loading indicators

Modal open/close status

Since these states don't belong to a specific component but affect layout and behavior globally, managing them via Vuex makes perfect sense.

```
// store/modules/ui.js
export default {
  namespaced: true,

  state: () => ({
    isSidebarOpen: true,
    darkMode: false
  }),

  getters: {
    sidebarState: (state) => state.isSidebarOpen,
```

```
    isDarkMode: (state) => state.darkMode
  },

  mutations: {
    TOGGLE_SIDEBAR(state) {
      state.isSidebarOpen = !state.isSidebarOpen
    },
    SET_DARK_MODE(state, value) {
      state.darkMode = value
    }
  },

  actions: {
    toggleSidebar({ commit }) {
      commit('TOGGLE_SIDEBAR')
    },
    enableDarkMode({ commit }) {
      commit('SET_DARK_MODE', true)
    },
    disableDarkMode({ commit }) {
      commit('SET_DARK_MODE', false)
    }
  }
}
```

Register it in the store:

```
import ui from './modules/ui'

export default createStore({
  modules: {
    ui
  }
})
```

And use it in your layout component:

```
<script setup>
import { useStore } from 'vuex'
import { computed } from 'vue'

const store = useStore()
```

```
const isSidebarOpen = computed(() =>
store.getters['ui/sidebarState'])

const toggleSidebar = () => {
  store.dispatch('ui/toggleSidebar')
}
</script>

<template>
  <div>
    <button @click="toggleSidebar">Toggle
Sidebar</button>
    <aside v-if="isSidebarOpen">Sidebar
Content</aside>
  </div>
</template>
```

This makes it easy to control layout behavior from any part of your app, especially when you need to sync UI interactions across components (like closing a sidebar from a modal or a route change).

In real applications, you need a reliable structure for:

Managing user authentication state, with login/logout and access control

Managing shopping cart state, including totals and item tracking

Managing UI state, like layout toggles and display settings

Vuex makes it possible to manage all of these using a centralized pattern that is predictable, scalable, and easy to test. By combining namespaced Vuex modules with Composition API components, you get a solution that:

Keeps logic organized

Encourages single responsibility per module

Promotes clean, readable component code

Supports reusability through composables and modular structure

This is a modern, production-ready way to handle shared state in Vue 3 applications.

Chapter 8: Navigating with Vue Router

One of the most powerful features of modern web applications is the ability to navigate between different parts of the application without refreshing the page. In a traditional multi-page app, every link click would reload a new HTML file from the server. But in Vue 3, we build single-page applications (SPAs), where routing happens entirely on the client side, and content updates dynamically.

Vue Router is the official routing library for Vue.js, designed specifically to integrate seamlessly with Vue 3 and the Composition API. It allows you to map URLs to components, control navigation flow, create dynamic route structures, protect views with authentication, and even optimize performance through lazy loading.

In this chapter, you'll learn how to configure and use Vue Router 4 for everything from simple page switching to advanced navigation guards and dynamic route matching. We'll also cover how routing integrates with the Composition API and how to use lifecycle hooks to control what happens during navigation.

Introduction to Vue Router 4

When you're building any modern Vue application that goes beyond a single view, you're going to need routing. That means having a way to navigate between views based on the URL in the address bar—without reloading the page. Whether you're showing a homepage, a user profile, a shopping cart, or a settings page, routing gives structure and flow to your app.

Vue Router is the tool Vue provides for this. And with Vue 3, we use **Vue Router 4**, which was designed from the ground up to work with Vue 3's Composition API, modern JavaScript patterns, and async component loading. It allows you to define routes, map them to components, react to route changes, guard routes based on authentication or other conditions, and control navigation behaviors in a clean and declarative way.

Installing Vue Router 4

To add Vue Router to your Vue 3 application, you install it using your package manager:

```
npm install vue-router@4
```

After installing, you create a router instance and register it with your app.

Creating Your First Router Configuration

Your router configuration is where you define which URLs map to which components.

Let's say your app has a homepage and an about page. You create two simple view components in the `src/views` directory:

```
<!-- views/Home.vue -->
<template>
  <h1>Home</h1>
</template>
<!-- views/About.vue -->
<template>
  <h1>About</h1>
</template>
```

Now you create the router configuration:

```
// router/index.js
import { createRouter, createWebHistory } from
'vue-router'
import Home from '@/views/Home.vue'
import About from '@/views/About.vue'

const routes = [
  { path: '/', component: Home },
  { path: '/about', component: About }
]

const router = createRouter({
  history: createWebHistory(),
  routes
})
```

```
export default router
```

The `createWebHistory()` function tells Vue Router to use the browser's native history API (pushState), which means you get clean URLs without hash symbols (e.g., `/about` instead of `/#/about`). If you're working in an environment that requires hash-based routing (e.g., GitHub Pages without server-side support), you can use `createWebHashHistory()` instead.

Registering the Router with the Application

Once the router is configured, you register it in your `main.js` file when setting up the app:

```
// main.js
import { createApp } from 'vue'
import App from './App.vue'
import router from './router'

const app = createApp(App)
app.use(router)
app.mount('#app')
```

This integrates the router with your Vue application and enables routing features like `<router-link>` and `<router-view>`.

Connecting URLs to Components

With routing configured, you can now build a layout with links that allow users to navigate between pages.

In your `App.vue`, add:

```
<template>
  <nav>
    <router-link to="/">Home</router-link>
    |
    <router-link to="/about">About</router-link>
  </nav>

  <main>
    <router-view />
  </main>
</template>
```

Here:

`<router-link>` replaces traditional `<a href="">` tags. It's reactive and works without reloading the page.

`<router-view>` is a placeholder that Vue Router will use to render the matched component for the current path.

When a user clicks on "About," Vue Router updates the URL and replaces the contents of `<router-view>` with the `About.vue` component—without refreshing the page.

Route Matching and URL Awareness

Vue Router watches the browser URL and matches it to the correct route. When the path changes (via clicking a link or using `router.push()`), it finds the route in your configuration and renders the associated component.

For example, if your route is defined as:

```
{ path: '/about', component: About }
```
Visiting `/about` in the browser will render the About view.

You can also control navigation programmatically using the `useRouter()` hook:

```
<script setup>
import { useRouter } from 'vue-router'

const router = useRouter()

const goToHome = () => {
  router.push('/')
}
</script>
```
This is useful in situations like form submissions or button clicks that should redirect the user after an event.

At this point, you have:

Installed and registered Vue Router

Defined basic static routes

Rendered route-linked views in your layout

Used `<router-link>` for navigation

Used `<router-view>` to display dynamic content

Learned how Vue Router keeps the interface in sync with the browser's URL

These are the foundational steps that allow your application to behave like a modern single-page app.

From here, we'll build on this knowledge to work with dynamic route parameters, query strings, nested routes for layouts, route guards for authentication, and hooks that let you run logic when navigation happens.

Let me know when you're ready for the next section on **Defining Routes,**

Defining Routes, Params, and Query Strings

In Vue Router, defining routes is about more than just connecting static paths to components. As your application becomes dynamic, you need to respond to data in the URL—like user IDs, product slugs, or search filters. Vue Router provides a clean and powerful way to access this kind of dynamic input through **route parameters** and **query strings**.

These two features—**params** and **queries**—let you capture and work with URL-based data in a way that keeps your app clean, flexible, and reactive. In this section, you'll learn how to define these routes, access their values, and build real-world interfaces around them using the Composition API.

Static Routes

Before adding dynamic data, start with a simple static route to anchor the concept.

```
const routes = [
  { path: '/', component: Home },
  { path: '/about', component: About }
]
```

These are fixed paths. Visiting `/about` will always show the same component. There's no room for variation or data coming from the URL itself.

But most real apps are not this static. You need to load different content depending on the route. For that, you use route parameters.

Route Parameters

Route parameters allow a path to accept **variable values**. For example, if you're building a blog, every post has a unique slug in the URL.

You define a dynamic route like this:

```
{ path: '/post/:slug', component: PostView }
```

Now, when the user visits `/post/hello-world`, Vue Router loads the `PostView` component and provides access to the `slug` parameter.

Inside the component, you access that parameter using the `useRoute()` hook:

```
<script setup>
import { useRoute } from 'vue-router'

const route = useRoute()
const slug = route.params.slug
</script>

<template>
  <h1>Viewing post: {{ slug }}</h1>
</template>
```

This value updates automatically if the route changes while the component is still mounted. Vue Router keeps it reactive, and you don't need to manually watch for changes unless you're fetching data based on it—which we'll get to shortly.

Example: Displaying User Profiles by ID

Suppose you're building a user management dashboard. You want a route like `/users/23` to show the profile for user #23.

Start by defining the route:

```
{ path: '/users/:id', component: () =>
import('@/views/UserProfile.vue') }
```

The `:id` is a **named parameter**, and you can use any name you like. You can also define multiple params like `/project/:projectId/task/:taskId`.

Then, in the `UserProfile.vue` component:

```
<script setup>
import { useRoute } from 'vue-router'
import { ref, watchEffect } from 'vue'

const route = useRoute()
const userId = route.params.id

const user = ref(null)

watchEffect(async () => {
  const res = await fetch(`/api/users/${userId}`)
  user.value = await res.json()
})
</script>

<template>
  <div v-if="user">
    <h2>{{ user.name }}</h2>
    <p>Email: {{ user.email }}</p>
    <p>Role: {{ user.role }}</p>
  </div>
  <p v-else>Loading...</p>
</template>
```

This is a complete solution that:

Responds to the URL dynamically

Fetches the correct data from the backend

Reactively updates the view if the route changes

If your component supports route updates (e.g., user ID changes while the component remains mounted), using `watchEffect()` ensures the data refreshes as needed.

231

Optional Route Params

You can make a parameter optional by adding a `?` after the param name:

```
{ path: '/products/:category?', component:
ProductList }
```

This allows the URL to match both `/products` and `/products/electronics`.

In your component:

```
const category = route.params.category || 'all'
```

Use this approach when you want a flexible URL structure that can adapt based on the presence or absence of a parameter.

Query Strings

In addition to params, Vue Router also handles **query strings**, which are often used for filters, search terms, pagination, or sorting options.

A URL with query strings looks like this:

```
/search?q=vue+3&page=2&sort=price
```

Here, the part after `?` is the query. In your route configuration, you don't need to define anything special. Vue Router will automatically parse and expose the query object.

Inside your component:

```
<script setup>
import { useRoute } from 'vue-router'

const route = useRoute()

const searchQuery = route.query.q
const page = route.query.page
const sort = route.query.sort || 'default'
</script>

<template>
  <h2>Search Results</h2>
```

```
  <p>Search: {{ searchQuery }}</p>
  <p>Page: {{ page }}</p>
  <p>Sorted by: {{ sort }}</p>
</template>
```

Queries are particularly useful when the parameters are optional, change frequently, or aren't a meaningful part of the route hierarchy.

Navigating with Params and Queries

To navigate to a route with params or queries, use `router.push()` programmatically.

Here's an example using both a path param and query string:

```
<script setup>
import { useRouter } from 'vue-router'

const router = useRouter()

const goToProduct = () => {
  router.push({
    path: '/product/42',
    query: { ref: 'homepage' }
  })
}
</script>

<template>
  <button @click="goToProduct">View
Product</button>
</template>
```

This sends the user to `/product/42?ref=homepage`.

Alternatively, if you want to construct a full path with variables:

```
router.push(`/product/${id}?ref=homepage`)
```

Both approaches are valid. The object form is easier to work with when handling dynamic query parameters programmatically.

Handling Param Changes with Lifecycle Awareness

One thing to keep in mind is that route parameters can change **without remounting the component**. This is common in views like UserProfile.vue, where the route stays matched but the user ID changes.

To respond to these updates properly, you can watch the param or use the onBeforeRouteUpdate() hook:

```
<script setup>
import { useRoute, onBeforeRouteUpdate } from 'vue-router'
import { ref } from 'vue'

const route = useRoute()
const userId = ref(route.params.id)
const user = ref(null)

const fetchUser = async (id) => {
  const res = await fetch(`/api/users/${id}`)
  user.value = await res.json()
}

await fetchUser(userId.value)

onBeforeRouteUpdate(async (to, from, next) => {
  userId.value = to.params.id
  await fetchUser(userId.value)
  next()
})
</script>
```

This ensures that if the URL changes from /users/23 to /users/24, the component doesn't need to reload, but it still fetches new data.

These tools allow you to build dynamic interfaces where the URL acts as a single source of truth. Whether you're building search pages, user profiles, filterable lists, or dashboards, understanding how to work with parameters and queries is key to building intuitive, flexible Vue applications.

Nested Routes and Route Guards

As your Vue application grows in complexity, you'll eventually need to organize routes that aren't just flat paths. Many real-world layouts—admin dashboards, tabbed interfaces, user areas—have components that serve as a structural shell, while child components are displayed within that shell depending on the route. This is where **nested routes** come into play.

At the same time, your application might also include areas that require access control, such as only allowing logged-in users to access certain views. That's where **route guards** are essential—they give you control over who can go where and under what conditions, all before navigation completes. Both of these features—nesting and guarding—are core to building reliable, user-aware routing structures in Vue applications

Nested Routes: Structuring Layouts with Children

Nested routes let you define a layout component (sometimes called a wrapper or shell), and render specific views inside that layout depending on the sub-path.

Here's a typical use case: an admin area with a sidebar that stays visible, and content that changes based on what the user selects—like /admin/users or /admin/settings.

You can define this structure by nesting child routes inside a parent route configuration:

```
// router/index.js
import { createRouter, createWebHistory } from
'vue-router'
import AdminLayout from '@/layouts/AdminLayout.vue'
import AdminUsers from
'@/views/admin/AdminUsers.vue'
import AdminSettings from
'@/views/admin/AdminSettings.vue'

const routes = [
  {
    path: '/admin',
    component: AdminLayout,
    children: [
      {
        path: 'users',
        component: AdminUsers
      },
```

```
      {
        path: 'settings',
        component: AdminSettings
      }
    ]
  }
]

const router = createRouter({
  history: createWebHistory(),
  routes
})

export default router
```

Here's how the layout component might look:

```
<!-- layouts/AdminLayout.vue -->
<template>
  <div class="admin-layout">
    <aside>
      <router-link to="/admin/users">Users</router-link>
      <router-link to="/admin/settings">Settings</router-link>
    </aside>
    <main>
      <router-view />
    </main>
  </div>
</template>
```

When the user visits `/admin/users`, **Vue Router renders** `AdminLayout.vue`, and inside the `<router-view>`, it loads `AdminUsers.vue`. The layout is persistent, and only the inner content changes.

This is extremely useful for:

Dashboards

Multi-tab interfaces

Role-specific areas of an app

236

Layouts that should remain visible across nested routes

You can also go deeper—nested routes can have nested routes of their own, forming a routing tree. Vue Router supports this without limitation.

Naming Nested Views (for Multi-View Layouts)

In more advanced cases, a layout may have **multiple `<router-view>` outlets**, and you can use **named views** to render different components into different sections of the layout.

Example:

```
{
  path: '/admin',
  components: {
    default: AdminMain,
    sidebar: AdminSidebar
  }
}
```

In the layout:

```
<router-view />
<router-view name="sidebar" />
```

This allows for highly flexible layouts where different components update independently based on the route.

Route Guards: Controlling Access to Routes

A **route guard** is a function that gets called before a route is entered or updated. It lets you cancel, redirect, or delay navigation based on any logic you need—like whether the user is authenticated, has a specific role, or has unsaved changes.

Vue Router supports several kinds of guards:

Global guards: run before any route

Per-route guards: defined in the route itself

In-component guards: inside a component that's being navigated to or away from

Global Before Guards

Global guards are added during router setup using `router.beforeEach()`. These run before any route is finalized.

```
// router/index.js
import store from '@/store'

router.beforeEach((to, from, next) => {
  const isAuthenticated =
store.getters['auth/isLoggedIn']

  if (to.meta.requiresAuth && !isAuthenticated) {
    next('/login') // redirect to login page
  } else {
    next() // allow navigation
  }
})
```

Then in your route config, mark protected routes with a meta field:

```
{
  path: '/dashboard',
  component: () => import('@/views/Dashboard.vue'),
  meta: { requiresAuth: true }
}
```

This keeps your protection logic centralized, clean, and reusable. You're not scattering access logic across every component.

Per-Route Guards

You can also define guards directly in the route configuration using `beforeEnter`:

```
{
  path: '/admin',
  component: AdminLayout,
  beforeEnter: (to, from, next) => {
    const hasAdminAccess =
store.getters['auth/isAdmin']
    if (!hasAdminAccess) {
      next('/not-authorized')
```

```
    } else {
      next()
    }
  }
}
```

This approach is useful when the access condition is tightly coupled to that specific route, rather than a general rule.

In-Component Guards

Sometimes you want to guard leaving a page—for example, if a form is partially filled and the user is about to navigate away without saving.

Vue Router supports onBeforeRouteLeave() inside the component:

```
<script setup>
import { onBeforeRouteLeave } from 'vue-router'

onBeforeRouteLeave((to, from, next) => {
  const confirmLeave = window.confirm('You have
unsaved changes. Leave anyway?')
  if (confirmLeave) {
    next()
  } else {
    next(false)
  }
})
</script>
```

This gives you granular control over navigation from within the component itself. It's very helpful for editing interfaces, multi-step wizards, or anything where data loss is a concern.

Combining Guards with Nested Routes

Nested routes and guards can be combined naturally. For example, you might want to protect all admin routes:

```
{
  path: '/admin',
  component: AdminLayout,
  meta: { requiresAuth: true },
```

```
  children: [
    { path: 'users', component: AdminUsers },
    { path: 'settings', component: AdminSettings }
  ]
}
```

The global guard can inspect `to.meta.requiresAuth`, and block access to all admin subroutes if the user isn't logged in. Since metadata cascades down, you can enforce access rules without repeating yourself.

Handling Redirects

Vue Router also supports automatic redirects based on routes or conditions.

Static redirect:

```
{ path: '/home', redirect: '/' }
```

Dynamic redirect using a function:

```
{
  path: '/legacy-route',
  redirect: (to) => {
    if (to.query.v === '2') return '/new-v2'
    return '/new'
  }
}
```

This is especially useful when migrating old route structures or providing backward compatibility.

Nested routes and route guards are essential tools in Vue Router that help structure your application for both layout and security.

Nested routes:

Let you build layout components with dynamic content inside them

Support multilevel navigation structures

Make interfaces like dashboards and sidebars easy to manage

Route guards:

Help control navigation flow based on authentication, roles, or app state

Let you prevent users from leaving pages prematurely

Centralize protection logic for better maintainability

Together, these features make it easy to design apps that are well-organized, secure, and user-aware—without bloated logic in your components or route definitions.

Dynamic Routing and Lazy Loading

When building modern Vue applications, there are two major concerns that often come up side-by-side: flexibility and performance. You want to define routes that are adaptable to data—such as products, users, or articles that each live at a different path—and you want your application to load quickly, even as it grows in size. Vue Router addresses both needs through **dynamic routing** and **lazy loading**.

These two features allow you to:

Define routes that react to URL parameters, like IDs or slugs

Load only the parts of your application that are needed when they are needed, keeping the initial load time fast

Understanding Dynamic Routing

Dynamic routing allows you to configure parts of your URL path to be variable. This is critical when you have hundreds or thousands of items—like blog posts or user profiles—each requiring a distinct page, but based on the same component logic.

To configure a dynamic route, you use a **parameter** in the path definition:

```
{
  path: '/product/:slug',
  component: ProductView
}
```

The :slug acts as a placeholder. It tells Vue Router, "this part of the path is dynamic, and its value should be made available to the component."

If a user navigates to `/product/macbook-pro`, the `ProductView` component will render, and inside that component, you can access the value `'macbook-pro'` via the `useRoute()` hook.

```
<script setup>
import { useRoute } from 'vue-router'

const route = useRoute()
const productSlug = route.params.slug
</script>

<template>
  <h1>Product Page</h1>
  <p>Slug: {{ productSlug }}</p>
</template>
```

This dynamic slug can then be used to fetch product data from a backend or load it from a client-side store.

Dynamic segments can be placed anywhere in the path:

```
{ path:
'/category/:categorySlug/product/:productId',
component: ProductDetails }
```

Now both `categorySlug` and `productId` will be available in `route.params`.

Lazy Loading Components

Lazy loading, or **code splitting**, means loading JavaScript components only when they're needed. Instead of bundling every route's component into your initial JavaScript bundle, you let Vue split them out so that only the route being visited is loaded.

This improves initial load time and performance—especially important on mobile devices or slow connections.

Vue Router supports lazy loading through **dynamic imports**.

Instead of:

```
import ProductView from '@/views/ProductView.vue'
```

```
{
  path: '/product/:slug',
  component: ProductView
}
```

You do this:

```
{
  path: '/product/:slug',
  component: () =>
import('@/views/ProductView.vue')
}
```

Vue will automatically create a separate JavaScript chunk for `ProductView.vue`, and only load it when a user visits a matching route.

This applies to any route component. Even top-level pages like `/login` or `/about` should be lazy-loaded in large applications.

Combining Dynamic Routing with Lazy Loading

You don't need to choose one or the other—**they're designed to work together.** In fact, combining them is where you gain the most value: flexible routes that only load when needed.

Let's build an example that brings both features together.

Directory Structure:

src/

  views/

    ProductView.vue

    CategoryView.vue

    NotFound.vue

  router/

    index.js

router/index.js:

```
import { createRouter, createWebHistory } from
'vue-router'

const routes = [
  {
    path: '/product/:slug',
    component: () =>
import('@/views/ProductView.vue')
  },
  {
    path: '/category/:categorySlug',
    component: () =>
import('@/views/CategoryView.vue')
  },
  {
    path: '/:pathMatch(.*)*',
    name: 'NotFound',
    component: () => import('@/views/NotFound.vue')
  }
]

const router = createRouter({
  history: createWebHistory(),
  routes
})

export default router
```

This configuration gives you:

Two dynamic routes (/product/:slug and /category/:categorySlug)

Lazy loading for both components

A catch-all 404 route for anything that doesn't match

Now, when a user navigates to /product/sony-headphones, Vue will:

Match the dynamic route

Load ProductView.vue only at that moment

Provide route.params.slug === 'sony-headphones' to the component

Inside the ProductView.vue Component

Let's show how to fetch dynamic data based on the slug:

```
<script setup>
import { useRoute } from 'vue-router'
import { ref, watchEffect } from 'vue'

const route = useRoute()
const product = ref(null)
const loading = ref(true)

watchEffect(async () => {
  loading.value = true
  const res = await
fetch(`/api/products/${route.params.slug}`)
  product.value = await res.json()
  loading.value = false
})
</script>

<template>
  <div v-if="loading">Loading product...</div>
  <div v-else-if="product">
    <h1>{{ product.name }}</h1>
    <p>{{ product.description }}</p>
    <p><strong>Price:</strong> ${{ product.price
}}</p>
  </div>
  <div v-else>
    <p>Product not found.</p>
  </div>
</template>
```

This logic:

Automatically responds when the route changes

Fetches the correct product data based on the URL

Handles loading and empty states gracefully

You can easily adapt this approach for users, posts, videos, or anything else that uses dynamic routing.

Route Aliases and Fallbacks

Vue Router also supports **aliases** and **wildcard matches**, which are useful when working with dynamic URLs and legacy systems.

For example:

```
{
  path: '/item/:id',
  alias: '/legacy-item/:id',
  component: () => import('@/views/ItemView.vue')
}
```

This allows both `/item/123` and `/legacy-item/123` to route to the same component.

You can also define wildcard fallback routes for non-existent paths:

```
{
  path: '/:pathMatch(.*)*',
  name: 'NotFound',
  component: () => import('@/views/NotFound.vue')
}
```

This ensures that 404 routes are handled gracefully and don't crash the app.

Practical Advice for Large Applications

As your app grows, you may end up with dozens of route-based components. Not all of them need to be in memory at once. Lazy loading helps you break up your application into smaller chunks so the browser only loads what's necessary.

Some common patterns:

Always lazy-load views (pages)

Avoid lazy-loading frequently reused UI components (like buttons or layout wrappers)

Group related routes using the same layout or module

Test your app with network throttling to verify the benefits

Webpack and Vite automatically handle chunking and caching, so you don't need to manage filenames or bundle logic manually.

Dynamic routes and lazy loading are essential techniques for building efficient, scalable Vue applications. Together, they allow your app to:

Respond to variable path segments like slugs or IDs

Load pages only when they are needed

Reduce the initial bundle size

Provide personalized experiences without unnecessary complexity

By taking advantage of these capabilities, you can ensure that your Vue application feels fast, stays maintainable, and responds dynamically to real user behavior.

Navigation Lifecycle and Hooks

In Vue Router, every time the URL changes, a process takes place behind the scenes before a new component is rendered. This process is known as the **navigation lifecycle**. It involves several steps where you, as the developer, can hook into the flow to perform logic: checking permissions, confirming with the user, fetching new data, cleaning up resources, or even canceling the navigation altogether.

Vue Router gives you multiple ways to tap into this flow using **navigation hooks**, which are callback functions that run at different points in the routing process. These hooks are essential for controlling user flow, managing asynchronous transitions, and ensuring that navigation is done safely and predictably.

Before Vue Router completes a navigation, it goes through a series of steps:

Trigger navigation (e.g., link click, `router.push`, back/forward button)

Run **global before hooks**

Run **per-route beforeEnter hooks**

Run **in-component `onBeforeRouteLeave` hooks**

Resolve new route and render component

Run **in-component** `onBeforeRouteUpdate` (if updating same component with new params)

Run **global after hooks**

At each stage, Vue Router gives you the opportunity to run logic or stop navigation.

Global Navigation Guards

These are hooks you register directly on the router instance. They apply to every route change and are often used for access control or global checks.

beforeEach – Guard Before Navigation Starts

```
// router/index.js
import { createRouter, createWebHistory } from
'vue-router'
import routes from './routes'
import store from '@/store'

const router = createRouter({
  history: createWebHistory(),
  routes
})

router.beforeEach((to, from, next) => {
  const isAuthenticated =
store.getters['auth/isLoggedIn']

  if (to.meta.requiresAuth && !isAuthenticated) {
    next('/login')
  } else {
    next()
  }
})
```

In this example:

If a route requires authentication and the user is not logged in, they are redirected to the login page.

Otherwise, navigation proceeds as normal.

Using `to.meta.requiresAuth` lets you declare authentication needs declaratively in route definitions:

```
{
  path: '/dashboard',
  component: () => import('@/views/Dashboard.vue'),
  meta: { requiresAuth: true }
}
```

`afterEach` – Runs After Navigation Completes

This is useful for side effects like analytics tracking:

```
router.afterEach((to, from) => {
  if (window.gtag) {
    window.gtag('event', 'page_view', {
      page_path: to.fullPath
    })
  }
})
```

It does not affect navigation—it's just for observing it.

Per-Route Guards

You can define a guard directly on a route definition using `beforeEnter`. This is best used when the logic is specific to that route.

```
{
  path: '/admin',
  component: () => import('@/views/Admin.vue'),
  beforeEnter: (to, from, next) => {
    const isAdmin = store.getters['auth/isAdmin']
    if (!isAdmin) {
      next('/not-authorized')
    } else {
      next()
    }
  }
}
```

The `beforeEnter` guard runs only when entering that specific route, and not when updating parameters within the same route. It's ideal for access control tied to a particular route group.

In-Component Guards with Composition API

Vue Router also provides hooks that live inside the component logic. These are helpful for scenarios like:

Prompting the user before leaving a form with unsaved changes

Reloading data when route parameters change

Cancelling navigation under certain conditions

Vue Router 4 provides `onBeforeRouteLeave` and `onBeforeRouteUpdate` hooks that you can use inside `<script setup>` or the regular setup function.

onBeforeRouteLeave

Use this when you want to prevent the user from accidentally leaving a page, especially when there's unsaved form data or ongoing uploads.

```
<script setup>
import { onBeforeRouteLeave } from 'vue-router'

onBeforeRouteLeave((to, from, next) => {
  const confirmLeave = window.confirm('You have
unsaved changes. Are you sure you want to leave?')
  if (confirmLeave) {
    next()
  } else {
    next(false) // cancel navigation
  }
})
</script>
```

This hook runs before navigating away from the current component.

onBeforeRouteUpdate

This is useful when the route changes but the same component remains mounted. It gives you a chance to react to param changes.

For example, if you're on `/user/1` and move to `/user/2`, and both use the same `UserProfile.vue` component, Vue will reuse the component instance and just update the route. This hook helps you react to that update.

```
<script setup>
import { onBeforeRouteUpdate, useRoute } from 'vue-
router'
import { ref } from 'vue'

const route = useRoute()
const user = ref(null)

const loadUser = async (id) => {
  const res = await fetch(`/api/users/${id}`)
  user.value = await res.json()
}

// Initial load
await loadUser(route.params.id)

onBeforeRouteUpdate(async (to, from, next) => {
  await loadUser(to.params.id)
  next()
})
</script>
```

This ensures the component updates with new data when the route changes, without forcing a full reload.

Cancelling and Redirecting Navigation

At any point in a guard, you can:

Allow navigation by calling `next()` (or just returning `true` in newer syntax)

Cancel navigation by calling `next(false)`

Redirect by passing a new location to `next()` or `return { path: '/somewhere' }`

Starting with Vue Router 4.1, you can also return promises or use async functions inside guards:

```
router.beforeEach(async (to, from) => {
```

```
  const isAllowed = await checkAccess(to)
  if (!isAllowed) {
    return '/login'
  }
})
```

This makes guards more intuitive and compatible with modern JavaScript.

Real-World Use Case: Blocking Navigation with Unsaved Form

Let's implement a complete example where a user is filling a form, and we want to prevent them from leaving without confirmation.

```
<script setup>
import { onBeforeRouteLeave } from 'vue-router'
import { ref } from 'vue'

const formData = ref({
  name: '',
  email: ''
})

const isDirty = ref(false)

function updateField(field, value) {
  formData.value[field] = value
  isDirty.value = true
}

onBeforeRouteLeave((to, from, next) => {
  if (isDirty.value) {
    const confirmLeave = window.confirm('You have
unsaved changes. Leave anyway?')
    if (confirmLeave) {
      next()
    } else {
      next(false)
    }
  } else {
    next()
  }
})
</script>
```

```
<template>
  <form>
    <input type="text" v-model="formData.name"
@input="updateField('name', $event.target.value)"
/>
    <input type="email" v-model="formData.email"
@input="updateField('email', $event.target.value)"
/>
  </form>
</template>
```

This protects against accidental data loss and shows how `onBeforeRouteLeave` fits naturally into component logic.

Navigation hooks in Vue Router give you deep control over the behavior of your application during routing changes. You've now seen how to:

Use global guards for authentication and analytics

Add per-route guards for route-specific access control

Write component-level hooks to prevent accidental exits or refresh data

Combine guards with async logic and route metadata

Mastering these tools allows you to control the user's experience with precision, handle edge cases gracefully, and build interfaces that feel polished and professional.

Chapter 9: Building and Connecting to APIs

Modern frontend applications are only as powerful as the data they can access. Whether you're building a blog, dashboard, e-commerce site, or admin tool, your Vue app will likely need to fetch, send, and sync data with a backend API. In Vue 3, especially with the Composition API, handling asynchronous data flows becomes much more streamlined—but it still requires a solid structure and practical strategy.

In this chapter, we'll work through the essentials of connecting your Vue app to external APIs. We'll start with how to fetch data using both Axios and the native Fetch API. We'll look at how to structure asynchronous code using `async/await`, how to manage errors and loading states gracefully, and how to encapsulate and reuse API logic across your application. We'll also explore how to handle both RESTful APIs and GraphQL endpoints in a Vue 3 application.

Fetching Data with Axios and the Fetch API

This is a foundational skill that connects your frontend application with backend services or external data providers. Whether you're pulling in a list of blog posts, submitting a form, or syncing user preferences, HTTP requests are the bridge between the browser and your server. And in a Vue 3 project using the Composition API, how you structure this interaction really matters for maintainability, reusability, and performance.

There are two widely used approaches when fetching data in Vue apps:

The native `fetch()` API, which is built into every modern browser

Third-party libraries like **Axios**, which simplify and enhance the process

Both work, and both are valid choices depending on your project's needs. We'll walk through both approaches in full context—showing how to use them inside Vue components, handle response data, and address common use cases such as setting headers and handling JSON.

Using the Fetch API in Vue 3

The `fetch()` function is a built-in browser feature that provides a modern, promise-based way to make HTTP requests. It's a good tool for quick and lightweight data retrieval, and it's widely supported.

Let's look at how to fetch a list of posts from a public API and render them in a Vue 3 component using the Composition API:

```
<script setup>
import { ref, onMounted } from 'vue'

const posts = ref([])
const loading = ref(true)
const error = ref(null)

onMounted(async () => {
  try {
    const response = await
fetch('https://jsonplaceholder.typicode.com/posts')

    if (!response.ok) {
      throw new Error(`Error ${response.status}:
${response.statusText}`)
    }

    const data = await response.json()
    posts.value = data
  } catch (err) {
    error.value = err.message
  } finally {
    loading.value = false
  }
})
</script>

<template>
  <div>
    <h2>Latest Posts</h2>
    <p v-if="loading">Loading posts...</p>
    <p v-else-if="error">{{ error }}</p>
    <ul v-else>
```

```
      <li v-for="post in posts" :key="post.id">
        {{ post.title }}
      </li>
    </ul>
  </div>
</template>
```

In this example:

We use `onMounted()` to trigger the fetch when the component is first rendered

We call `response.json()` to convert the raw response into a usable JavaScript object

We use reactive `ref()`s to handle the state of our data, error, and loading status

This setup works well for basic GET requests. However, the native `fetch()` function does require a bit more manual handling—like checking for HTTP errors yourself and setting headers when sending data.

Sending Data with Fetch (POST Example)

If you want to send data using a POST request, you need to set headers and include the body explicitly.

Here's a basic example of sending a new comment:

```
const newComment = {
  postId: 1,
  name: 'Alex',
  body: 'This is a test comment'
}

const response = await
fetch('https://jsonplaceholder.typicode.com/comment
s', {
  method: 'POST',
  headers: {
    'Content-Type': 'application/json'
  },
  body: JSON.stringify(newComment)
})

const result = await response.json()
```

```
console.log(result)
```

You always need to stringify the request body and set the `Content-Type` to `'application/json'` when sending JSON.

Using Axios in Vue 3

Axios is a robust and developer-friendly HTTP client. It handles many of the things that `fetch()` leaves to you—automatic JSON parsing, status code validation, request timeouts, and more.

To get started with Axios in a Vue 3 project:

```
npm install axios
```

Then import and use it like this:

```
<script setup>
import { ref, onMounted } from 'vue'
import axios from 'axios'

const users = ref([])
const loading = ref(true)
const error = ref(null)

onMounted(async () => {
  try {
    const response = await
axios.get('https://jsonplaceholder.typicode.com/use
rs')
    users.value = response.data
  } catch (err) {
    error.value = err.message || 'Something went
wrong'
  } finally {
    loading.value = false
  }
})
</script>

<template>
  <div>
    <h2>Users</h2>
```

```
    <p v-if="loading">Loading users...</p>
    <p v-else-if="error">{{ error }}</p>
    <ul v-else>
      <li v-for="user in users" :key="user.id">{{
user.name }}</li>
    </ul>
  </div>
</template>
```

Notice how much cleaner the Axios syntax is:

It automatically parses the JSON response (`response.data`)

It throws on non-200 responses (so you don't have to check `.ok`)

It includes full request and response details in the error object, which helps with debugging

POST Request with Axios

Sending a POST request with Axios is also cleaner:

```
const newPost = {
  title: 'New Post',
  body: 'This is the content of the post',
  userId: 1
}

const response = await
axios.post('https://jsonplaceholder.typicode.com/po
sts', newPost)
console.log(response.data)
```

No need to stringify the body or manually set headers—Axios handles that for you automatically when sending JSON.

Adding Authorization Headers

If you need to include an authorization token or other headers, you can pass them as the third argument to `axios.get()` or second argument to `axios.post()`:

```
const token = 'abc123'
```

```
const response = await axios.get('/api/private', {
  headers: {
    Authorization: `Bearer ${token}`
  }
})
```

You can also set default headers globally using an Axios instance (which we'll cover more when we build a reusable API service).

Fetch vs Axios: When to Use Which?

Both tools can handle your HTTP needs, but the decision often comes down to trade-offs between control and convenience.

Use **Axios** if you want easier error handling, JSON parsing, interceptors, timeouts, and broader feature support.

Use **Fetch** if you want to avoid third-party dependencies and you're comfortable handling things like status code checks and request configuration manually.

In production-grade applications, Axios tends to be preferred due to its feature set and clean syntax.

Whether you use Axios or the native Fetch API, what matters most is understanding how to structure your data flows clearly and predictably within Vue 3's Composition API.

Handling Asynchronous Requests

When your application needs to communicate with a backend, those interactions often happen asynchronously. Whether you're loading a list of records, submitting a form, fetching data when a route changes, or polling for updates, asynchronous requests are at the core of frontend development. The challenge isn't just making the request—it's structuring that logic in a way that's responsive, resilient, and easy to maintain.

In Vue 3, especially when using the Composition API, handling asynchronous behavior becomes more flexible. But with that flexibility comes the responsibility to manage state transitions, avoid race conditions, and handle user interaction in real time.

Let's now explore how to handle asynchronous requests properly using Vue 3's reactivity system, lifecycle hooks, and utility patterns that help you manage complex flows without compromising readability or performance.

Asynchronous Data with Lifecycle Hooks

One of the most common use cases is loading data when a component is mounted. You typically do this inside onMounted() using an async function.

```
<script setup>
import { ref, onMounted } from 'vue'
import axios from 'axios'

const posts = ref([])
const loading = ref(false)
const error = ref(null)

onMounted(async () => {
  loading.value = true
  error.value = null

  try {
    const response = await
axios.get('https://jsonplaceholder.typicode.com/pos
ts')
    posts.value = response.data
  } catch (err) {
    error.value = 'Failed to load posts.'
  } finally {
    loading.value = false
  }
})
</script>
```

This structure ensures:

You communicate the loading state to the user

Errors are caught and handled gracefully

Data is stored in a reactive variable

All of this is part of creating an experience that is predictable and user-friendly.

Reacting to Changing Inputs with `watch`

Sometimes you need to perform a new request when a specific value changes—such as a route parameter, a selected dropdown value, or a search input.

Vue's `watch()` function allows you to respond reactively to these changes:

```
<script setup>
import { ref, watch } from 'vue'
import axios from 'axios'

const searchQuery = ref('')
const results = ref([])

watch(searchQuery, async (newQuery) => {
  if (newQuery.length < 3) {
    results.value = []
    return
  }

  try {
    const res = await
axios.get(`https://api.example.com/search?q=${newQuery}`)
    results.value = res.data
  } catch (err) {
    console.error('Search failed:', err)
  }
})
</script>
```

In this example, the app responds to user input in real time. The moment the query string changes, a new request is sent. But you also want to ensure:

You don't send a request for empty or short input

You handle failures without breaking the UI

This pattern is useful in search boxes, filters, or dashboard widgets where the data should update automatically.

Preventing Race Conditions

Let's say a user types quickly into a search box, and each keystroke triggers a request. The responses might arrive out of order. That means your results list could show outdated data from an earlier request.

To avoid this, you can use a request counter or a cancellation token.

Here's an approach using a request ID:

```
<script setup>
import { ref, watch } from 'vue'
import axios from 'axios'

const query = ref('')
const results = ref([])
let requestId = 0

watch(query, async (value) => {
  if (value.length < 2) return

  const currentRequest = ++requestId

  try {
    const res = await
axios.get(`/api/search?q=${value}`)

    if (currentRequest === requestId) {
      results.value = res.data
    }
  } catch (err) {
    console.error('Error fetching search results:',
err)
  }
})
</script>
```

Each time a new request is triggered, we increment `requestId`. Only the response from the latest request will be used. This is a lightweight way to maintain data integrity in high-frequency updates.

Aborting Requests with `AbortController` (Fetch Only)

If you're using the native `fetch()` API, you can cancel in-progress requests with `AbortController`.

```
let controller = null

watch(query, async (value) => {
  if (controller) controller.abort()
  controller = new AbortController()

  try {
    const response = await
fetch(`/api/search?q=${value}`, {
      signal: controller.signal
    })
    const data = await response.json()
    results.value = data
  } catch (err) {
    if (err.name !== 'AbortError') {
      console.error('Request failed:', err)
    }
  }
})
```

This ensures that only the most recent request continues, and any older requests are canceled before they complete. Axios also supports request cancellation through the `CancelToken` API (deprecated) or the native `AbortController` in modern versions.

Sequencing Requests

In many cases, one request depends on the result of another. For example, you might need to fetch user details first, and then load their permissions.

```
<script setup>
import { ref, onMounted } from 'vue'
import axios from 'axios'
```

263

```
const user = ref(null)
const permissions = ref([])

onMounted(async () => {
  try {
    const res1 = await axios.get('/api/user')
    user.value = res1.data

    const res2 = await
axios.get(`/api/users/${user.value.id}/permissions`
)
    permissions.value = res2.data
  } catch (err) {
    console.error('Request chain failed:', err)
  }
})
</script>
```

This pattern ensures the second request only runs after the first one has succeeded. Be sure to structure this carefully so that if the first call fails, you don't try to access properties from user.value that don't exist.

Using watchEffect for Immediate Reactive Data Fetching

If you want to fetch data reactively based on a combination of dependencies and have the logic run immediately on first render, watchEffect() is a good choice:

```
<script setup>
import { ref, watchEffect } from 'vue'
import axios from 'axios'

const selectedUserId = ref(1)
const userDetails = ref(null)

watchEffect(async () => {
  try {
    const res = await
axios.get(`/api/users/${selectedUserId.value}`)
    userDetails.value = res.data
  } catch (err) {
```

```
      console.error('User fetch failed:', err)
    }
})
</script>
```

The request runs immediately and re-runs automatically when `selectedUserId` changes. This is useful when the dependencies are simple and the logic is straightforward.

Handling Multiple Simultaneous Requests

You might also need to load several independent pieces of data at once—such as dashboard metrics, notifications, and user preferences.

```
<script setup>
import { ref, onMounted } from 'vue'
import axios from 'axios'

const metrics = ref(null)
const notifications = ref(null)
const preferences = ref(null)

onMounted(async () => {
  try {
    const [metricsRes, notificationsRes, prefsRes]
= await Promise.all([
      axios.get('/api/dashboard/metrics'),
      axios.get('/api/notifications'),
      axios.get('/api/user/preferences')
    ])

    metrics.value = metricsRes.data
    notifications.value = notificationsRes.data
    preferences.value = prefsRes.data
  } catch (err) {
    console.error('One or more requests failed:',
err)
  }
})
</script>
```

Using `Promise.all()` is efficient because it runs all requests in parallel and only waits for all to complete. If any request fails, the `catch` block will be triggered.

When it comes to handling asynchronous requests in Vue 3, the key is to be deliberate and thoughtful about state management, user experience, and logic sequencing.

You now understand how to:

Fetch data on component mount using `onMounted()`

React to changes in state or route using `watch()` and `watchEffect()`

Avoid race conditions using counters or `AbortController`

Chain requests safely when one depends on the other

Handle loading and error states to improve UX

Fire multiple requests simultaneously and manage their responses

These techniques prepare you to build data-driven applications that are responsive, consistent, and user-focused.

Error Handling and Loading States

When you're building Vue applications that depend on data from external sources, you're dealing with systems you don't control. That means network requests can fail, slow down, or return unexpected results. Your app must handle these situations gracefully—otherwise, users are left with broken screens, confusing behavior, or no feedback at all. To build a reliable interface, you need to provide visual cues during loading and clearly handle errors when they occur.

In Vue 3, you have full control over how you track and present both the loading process and any errors that come up. These aren't just nice-to-have UI features—they're essential to providing a responsive and trustworthy user experience.

The Basics: Tracking Loading and Error State

When making an asynchronous request, you want to track three distinct states:

`loading`: whether the operation is currently in progress

`error`: whether the operation failed

`data`: the successful result, if the operation succeeds

All three of these should be declared as reactive references so that your template can update automatically.

```
<script setup>
import { ref, onMounted } from 'vue'
import axios from 'axios'

const users = ref([])
const loading = ref(false)
const error = ref(null)

onMounted(async () => {
  loading.value = true
  error.value = null

  try {
    const res = await
axios.get('https://jsonplaceholder.typicode.com/use
rs')
    users.value = res.data
  } catch (err) {
    error.value = 'Failed to load users.'
  } finally {
    loading.value = false
  }
})
</script>

<template>
  <div>
    <p v-if="loading">Loading users...</p>
    <p v-else-if="error">{{ error }}</p>
    <ul v-else>
      <li v-for="user in users" :key="user.id">
        {{ user.name }}
```

```
        </li>
      </ul>
    </div>
  </template>
```

This setup ensures that:

While the request is being processed, the UI displays a loading indicator

If an error occurs, the user sees a clear message

Only when data is successfully retrieved will the content render

This is the simplest and cleanest way to handle loading and error states in Vue 3, and you can apply this pattern across components.

Making Error Messages Meaningful

It's important to give users feedback that they understand. A raw error object or HTTP code like ERR_NETWORK doesn't mean much to an end user. You should translate technical errors into helpful messages.

Here's how you might expand your error handling logic:

```
try {
  const res = await axios.get('/api/data')
  data.value = res.data
} catch (err) {
  if (!err.response) {
    error.value = 'Network error: Please check your
connection.'
  } else if (err.response.status === 404) {
    error.value = 'Data not found.'
  } else if (err.response.status === 500) {
    error.value = 'Server error. Please try again
later.'
  } else {
    error.value = 'An unexpected error occurred.'
  }
}
```

By tailoring messages to the context, you help users understand what went wrong and how they might respond—retrying later, refreshing the page, or reporting a bug.

Showing and Hiding Loading Indicators

A good loading indicator does two things:

Lets users know that something is happening

Prevents confusion or accidental repeated actions

You can place a loading spinner or text in place of content, or you can overlay it if the layout needs to stay visible.

Example:

```
<template>
  <div class="card">
    <div class="spinner" v-
if="loading">Loading...</div>
    <div v-else>
      <h2>{{ post.title }}</h2>
      <p>{{ post.body }}</p>
    </div>
  </div>
</template>
```

You can also use conditional classes to dim content or disable interactions during loading:

```
<template>
  <div :class="{ 'dimmed': loading }">
    <form @submit.prevent="submit">
      <input v-model="form.title" />
      <button :disabled="loading">Submit</button>
    </form>
    <p v-if="loading">Submitting...</p>
  </div>
</template>

<style scoped>
.dimmed {
  opacity: 0.5;
  pointer-events: none;
}
</style>
```

This makes it clear to the user that the app is working and that they should wait.

Centralizing Loading and Error Handling in Composables

To keep your components clean, you can move loading/error logic into reusable **composables**.

Let's say you have a composable that loads a list of products:

```js
// composables/useProducts.js
import { ref } from 'vue'
import axios from 'axios'

export function useProducts() {
  const products = ref([])
  const loading = ref(false)
  const error = ref(null)

  const fetchProducts = async () => {
    loading.value = true
    error.value = null

    try {
      const res = await axios.get('/api/products')
      products.value = res.data
    } catch (err) {
      error.value = 'Could not load products.'
    } finally {
      loading.value = false
    }
  }

  return {
    products,
    loading,
    error,
    fetchProducts
  }
}
```

Then use it inside your component:

```
<script setup>
import { onMounted } from 'vue'
import { useProducts } from
'@/composables/useProducts'

const { products, loading, error, fetchProducts } =
useProducts()

onMounted(fetchProducts)
</script>
```

This approach:

Keeps your logic modular and testable

Makes components easier to read

Encourages reuse across multiple views

Real-World Scenario: API Failures and Retry

Let's say you're loading data for a dashboard, but the API call fails due to a timeout or temporary issue. You want to show a retry button.

```
<template>
  <div>
    <p v-if="loading">Loading dashboard...</p>
    <p v-else-if="error">
      {{ error }}
      <button @click="loadDashboard">Retry</button>
    </p>
    <div v-else>
      <!-- dashboard data -->
    </div>
  </div>
</template>

<script setup>
import { ref } from 'vue'
import axios from 'axios'

const dashboard = ref(null)
const loading = ref(false)
const error = ref(null)
```

```
const loadDashboard = async () => {
  loading.value = true
  error.value = null

  try {
    const res = await axios.get('/api/dashboard')
    dashboard.value = res.data
  } catch (err) {
    error.value = 'Dashboard could not be loaded.
Please try again.'
  } finally {
    loading.value = false
  }
}

loadDashboard()
</script>
```

This gives the user control and trust in the application's behavior—even when things go wrong.

Errors and loading states are not just technical concerns—they directly affect how users experience your app. By explicitly handling them, you create a more resilient and predictable interface.

Building a Reusable API Service

As your application grows, you'll find yourself repeating the same logic in multiple components—sending GET requests, posting data, attaching headers, managing error handling, and dealing with response parsing. If each component handles these concerns independently, you quickly end up with duplicated logic, inconsistent behavior, and difficulty in maintaining or testing your code.

A cleaner and more scalable approach is to **centralize your API interactions** in a single, reusable module. This abstraction allows you to:

Apply global configurations like base URLs and headers

Handle errors in one place

Organize endpoints logically by domain or feature

Simplify component code and make it more focused

Step 1: Creating an Axios Instance

Start by creating an Axios instance with a default configuration that applies to all requests.

```
// services/api.js
import axios from 'axios'

const api = axios.create({
  baseURL: 'https://jsonplaceholder.typicode.com',
  timeout: 10000,
  headers: {
    'Content-Type': 'application/json'
  }
})

export default api
```

This instance is now your central HTTP client. You can reuse it throughout your application, and it will automatically use the base URL and default headers you configured.

You can also apply interceptors here for request logging, auth tokens, or global error handling.

Step 2: Handling Authentication Automatically (Optional)

If your app requires a token to access protected endpoints, you can add that logic directly to the Axios instance. For example:

```
// services/api.js (continued)

api.interceptors.request.use(config => {
  const token = localStorage.getItem('auth_token')
  if (token) {
    config.headers.Authorization = `Bearer ${token}`
  }
  return config
```

```
})
```

This ensures that every request includes the auth token automatically, without needing to pass it manually in each component.

Step 3: Creating Domain-Specific API Modules

Now that you have a reusable API client, organize your endpoints by feature. Let's say you have `posts`, `users`, and `comments`.

You can create individual files for each API domain:

```
// services/posts.js
import api from './api'

export function getAllPosts() {
  return api.get('/posts')
}

export function getPost(id) {
  return api.get(`/posts/${id}`)
}

export function createPost(data) {
  return api.post('/posts', data)
}

export function updatePost(id, data) {
  return api.put(`/posts/${id}`, data)
}

export function deletePost(id) {
  return api.delete(`/posts/${id}`)
}
```

Each function wraps an HTTP call, making it easy to use in your components without worrying about the underlying URL, headers, or method.

This modular approach mirrors how you organize your features. Each module is:

Focused on a specific resource

Easy to test and mock

Reusable across multiple views

Step 4: Using the API Module in a Component

Here's how you can consume these services in a Vue component:

```
<script setup>
import { ref, onMounted } from 'vue'
import { getAllPosts } from '@/services/posts'

const posts = ref([])
const loading = ref(false)
const error = ref(null)

onMounted(async () => {
  loading.value = true
  try {
    const response = await getAllPosts()
    posts.value = response.data
  } catch (err) {
    error.value = 'Failed to fetch posts.'
  } finally {
    loading.value = false
  }
})
</script>

<template>
  <div>
    <h2>All Posts</h2>
    <p v-if="loading">Loading...</p>
    <p v-else-if="error">{{ error }}</p>
    <ul v-else>
      <li v-for="post in posts" :key="post.id">{{
post.title }}</li>
    </ul>
  </div>
</template>
```

By abstracting the HTTP logic into a separate service file, your component becomes easier to read, more focused on presentation, and easier to maintain.

Step 5: Global Error Interceptor (Optional but Practical)

Sometimes, you want to handle certain errors globally—such as redirecting to login on `401 Unauthorized`, showing a toast on `500 Server Error`, or tracking failed requests.

Axios interceptors allow this:

```js
// services/api.js (continued)

api.interceptors.response.use(
  response => response,
  error => {
    if (error.response) {
      const { status } = error.response

      if (status === 401) {
        window.location.href = '/login'
      }

      if (status === 500) {
        console.error('A server error occurred.')
      }
    }

    return Promise.reject(error)
  }
)
```

This avoids repeating the same error logic in every component, and makes your API service more robust.

Step 6: Testing and Mocking the Service

Because your components use isolated API modules, you can mock these in tests without mocking Axios directly.

Example using Jest:

```js
// __mocks__/posts.js
export function getAllPosts() {
  return Promise.resolve({
    data: [
```

```
      { id: 1, title: 'Mock Post 1' },
      { id: 2, title: 'Mock Post 2' }
    ]
  })
}
```

In your test setup:

```
jest.mock('@/services/posts', () =>
require('__mocks__/posts'))
```

This lets you unit test components with predictable, isolated behavior—without making real HTTP requests.

A reusable API service transforms how you build and scale Vue applications. It brings order, consistency, and control to a part of your app that is often overlooked until it becomes a mess.

By creating an Axios instance, organizing endpoints into logical modules, and handling concerns like auth and errors centrally, you give your project a solid backbone for every data interaction.

Working with REST and GraphQL

Connecting your Vue 3 application to a backend API is at the core of any serious frontend development. Whether you're displaying a list of products, retrieving a user's profile, or submitting a form, you're talking to a server that serves data. The way your application interacts with the server depends largely on the architecture of the API you're working with.

Most APIs fall into two categories:

REST (Representational State Transfer), which uses structured URLs and standard HTTP verbs

GraphQL, which uses a single endpoint and allows the client to specify exactly what data it needs

Each has its own strengths and trade-offs. In this section, you'll learn how to work effectively with both REST and GraphQL APIs in Vue 3 using the

Composition API, how to manage requests, and how to build flexible, maintainable code around either architecture.

Integrating with REST APIs in Vue 3

A REST API exposes a collection of endpoints that correspond to resources. Each resource can be fetched, created, updated, or deleted using standard HTTP methods.

For example, in a typical REST setup, you might have endpoints like:

GET /users — get all users

GET /users/42 — get user with ID 42

POST /users — create a new user

PUT /users/42 — update user 42

DELETE /users/42 — delete user 42

Let's see how to work with this pattern using Axios and the Composition API.

Here's a real example of fetching a list of posts from a REST API:

```
<script setup>
import { ref, onMounted } from 'vue'
import axios from 'axios'

const posts = ref([])
const loading = ref(false)
const error = ref(null)

onMounted(async () => {
  loading.value = true
  try {
    const res = await
axios.get('https://jsonplaceholder.typicode.com/pos
ts')
    posts.value = res.data
  } catch (err) {
    error.value = 'Unable to fetch posts.'
  } finally {
```

```
        loading.value = false
    }
})
</script>

<template>
  <div>
    <h2>Blog Posts</h2>
    <p v-if="loading">Loading...</p>
    <p v-else-if="error">{{ error }}</p>
    <ul v-else>
      <li v-for="post in posts" :key="post.id">{{
post.title }}</li>
    </ul>
  </div>
</template>
```

This is a complete REST call cycle:

It uses GET to fetch a list of resources.

It handles loading and error states reactively.

It cleanly updates the UI when data is received.

For operations like POST and PUT, you'd use `axios.post()` or `axios.put()` in a similar pattern.

REST is stateless, well-documented, and predictable. Most public APIs and traditional backends use this model. But there are situations where REST becomes inefficient—for example, when you need deeply nested or partial data.

That's where GraphQL shines.

Integrating with GraphQL APIs in Vue 3

GraphQL changes how you think about fetching data. Instead of hitting multiple endpoints to gather information, the client sends a single query to one endpoint and specifies exactly what fields it wants.

A typical GraphQL request looks like this:

```
query {
```

```
  user(id: "42") {
    name
    email
    posts {
      id
      title
    }
  }
}
```

The server responds with only that data. You don't get extra fields, and you don't have to make additional requests to get related data. It's especially useful in mobile or frontend-heavy applications where minimizing over-fetching and request count is important.

Installing graphql-request

While there are larger GraphQL clients like Apollo, if you want a minimal and effective solution, graphql-request is a great tool. It's lightweight and works well with the Composition API.

Install it first:

```
npm install graphql-request
Then set up a basic client:
// services/graphql.js
import { GraphQLClient } from 'graphql-request'

export const graphql = new
GraphQLClient('https://api.example.com/graphql', {
  headers: {
    Authorization: `Bearer
${localStorage.getItem('auth_token')}`
  }
})
```

Now let's create a query:

```
// services/queries.js
export const GET_USER_WITH_POSTS = `
  query getUser($id: ID!) {
    user(id: $id) {
      name
```

```
      email
      posts {
        id
        title
      }
    }
  }
```

And then consume it in a Vue component:

```
<script setup>
import { ref, onMounted } from 'vue'
import { graphql } from '@/services/graphql'
import { GET_USER_WITH_POSTS } from
'@/services/queries'

const user = ref(null)
const loading = ref(false)
const error = ref(null)

onMounted(async () => {
  loading.value = true
  try {
    const data = await
graphql.request(GET_USER_WITH_POSTS, { id: '42' })
    user.value = data.user
  } catch (err) {
    error.value = 'Could not load user.'
  } finally {
    loading.value = false
  }
})
</script>

<template>
  <div>
    <h2>User Profile</h2>
    <p v-if="loading">Loading...</p>
    <p v-else-if="error">{{ error }}</p>
    <div v-else>
      <h3>{{ user.name }}</h3>
      <p>{{ user.email }}</p>
```

```
      <h4>Posts:</h4>
      <ul>
        <li v-for="post in user.posts"
:key="post.id">{{ post.title }}</li>
      </ul>
    </div>
  </div>
</template>
```

This example illustrates the key strengths of GraphQL:

One request returns user info and associated posts

No need to make separate API calls or manage dependencies between them

You fetch exactly what you need

Mutations with GraphQL

To change data (create, update, delete), you use **mutations** instead of queries.

Here's a mutation to create a post:

```
export const CREATE_POST = `
  mutation createPost($input: CreatePostInput!) {
    createPost(input: $input) {
      id
      title
      body
    }
  }
`
```

And here's how to call it:

```
const newPost = {
  title: 'Vue and GraphQL',
  body: 'This post was created using a GraphQL
mutation.'
}

await graphql.request(CREATE_POST, { input: newPost
})
```

GraphQL's flexibility shines here as well. You can ask for only the fields you care about in the response and combine related operations if the schema supports it.

Choosing Between REST and GraphQL

Both REST and GraphQL are useful. Which one to use depends on the nature of the project and the capabilities of the backend you're working with.

Use **REST** when:

You're consuming a stable, resource-oriented API

Your data model maps well to CRUD operations

You value simplicity and standard HTTP semantics

Use **GraphQL** when:

You need flexibility in the shape of data returned

You're working with deeply nested or connected data

You want fewer requests and more efficiency over the wire

You don't need to pick one exclusively. Some applications use REST for most backend interactions and reserve GraphQL for specific views or features where it adds value.

Combining Both Approaches

In a real-world scenario, your application might use REST for core user and session management, and GraphQL for fetching business-specific data like analytics, search results, or product listings.

You can structure your Vue project with both in mind:

```
src/

  services/

    api.js          ← Axios instance for REST

    graphql.js      ← GraphQL client

    users.js        ← REST API functions
```

```
posts.js          ← REST or GraphQL

queries.js        ← GraphQL queries and mutations
```

This separation makes your app flexible and prepared for change. If a REST endpoint is later replaced by a GraphQL one, you only update the service module—not your components.

Vue 3 works seamlessly with both REST and GraphQL. Understanding how to structure your data layer around each approach helps you write clean, scalable, and resilient code.

Chapter 10: Real-World App Development and Deployment

Now that you've learned the building blocks of Vue 3—Components, Composition API, Vue Router, Vuex (or Pinia), and API integration—the next step is to bring everything together in a cohesive, full-featured application. This chapter focuses on what it takes to go from individual features to a fully working, deployable product.

You'll learn how to plan and organize your application architecture, integrate your core modules (state, routing, logic), implement authentication securely, and finally deploy your Vue application to a live hosting platform like Netlify, Vercel, or Firebase.

Planning the Application Structure

When you're building a serious Vue 3 application—something more complex than a simple counter or form—you need to think carefully about how everything is organized. The bigger your app becomes, the more important structure becomes, because it's what keeps your code maintainable, modular, and easy for other developers (and your future self) to understand.

You don't want to end up with a project that feels like a tangle of components, state, and logic crammed into random folders. A well-planned structure gives you predictability, separation of concerns, scalability, and testability. It also makes onboarding new developers much smoother, because everything is in its right place.

Organizing by Function, Not Just Type

At the core of any scalable structure is the idea that your files should be grouped by what they **do**, not just by what they **are**. Grouping by file type might seem natural at first (e.g., putting all components in one folder, all views in another), but over time it becomes harder to maintain.

Let's say you have a blog with posts, users, and comments. If you put all your .vue files into a single `components/` directory, it'll quickly become unclear what each one belongs to.

A better approach is to organize by **feature** or **domain**. That way, every feature lives in its own directory with its views, components, store, API, and tests. This keeps related files together and reduces cognitive load.

A Practical Example: Scalable Project Structure

Let's go through a sample structure you might use for a dashboard-style Vue app that includes authentication, user profiles, and a product catalog:

```
src/
├── main.js
├── App.vue
│
├── assets/              → Global styles, images, fonts
├── components/          → Truly reusable UI elements
(buttons, inputs, modals)
├── layouts/             → Layout shells like AuthLayout,
DashboardLayout
├── router/              → Route definitions and guards
├── store/               → Vuex modules or Pinia stores
├── services/            → API wrappers (Axios, GraphQL
clients, etc.)
├── composables/         → Reusable logic (useAuth, useForm,
usePagination)
├── views/               → Page components that map to
routes
│   ├── auth/
│   │   ├── LoginView.vue
│   │   └── RegisterView.vue
```

```
|     ├── dashboard/
|     |     └── DashboardHome.vue
|     └── users/
|           ├── UserListView.vue
|           └── UserDetailView.vue
|
├── modules/              → Feature domains with everything
encapsulated
|     ├── products/
|     |     ├── ProductListView.vue
|     |     ├── ProductDetailView.vue
|     |     ├── productStore.js
|     |     └── productService.js
|     └── orders/
|           ├── OrderListView.vue
|           ├── OrderDetailView.vue
|           ├── orderStore.js
|           └── orderService.js
└── utils/                → Pure functions, date formatters,
constants
```

This kind of structure serves both small and large teams well. You still have central folders for shared code (components/, services/, composables/), but each domain feature—like products/ or orders/—manages itself. You can easily locate the service or store tied to a specific feature without searching through generic folders.

Keeping Components Focused

It helps to define a clear line between a **view** and a **component**.

A **view** is tied to a route (`/dashboard`, `/users/:id`) and often includes layout decisions or page-level logic.

A **component** is a reusable unit of UI, like a dropdown, card, or button. It should do one thing well and not know anything about routing or global state unless necessary.

For example:

```vue
<!-- components/UserCard.vue -->
<template>
  <div class="user-card">
    <img :src="user.avatar" />
    <p>{{ user.name }}</p>
  </div>
</template>

<script setup>
defineProps({
  user: Object
})
</script>
```

This is a reusable component. It might appear in multiple views—`UserListView.vue`, `AdminDashboard.vue`, and even `CommentSection.vue`. Views can then bring these components together, manage route-specific data fetching, and determine what gets displayed.

Managing Layouts

Most real-world apps have different layouts for different sections. You might have:

An authenticated dashboard layout (with sidebar and header)

A public layout for login and register pages

A blank layout for print or fullscreen views

A flexible way to manage this is by creating layout components like `DashboardLayout.vue` or `AuthLayout.vue` and wrapping your views accordingly.

For example:

```vue
<!-- layouts/DashboardLayout.vue -->
<template>
  <div class="dashboard-layout">
    <Sidebar />
    <Header />
    <main>
      <slot />
    </main>
  </div>
</template>
```

Then in your routes:

```js
{
  path: '/dashboard',
  component: DashboardLayout,
  children: [
    {
      path: '',
      name: 'DashboardHome',
      component: () =>
import('@/views/dashboard/DashboardHome.vue')
    },
    {
      path: 'users',
      name: 'UserList',
      component: () =>
import('@/views/users/UserListView.vue')
    }
  ]
}
```

This approach allows you to keep the layout shell in place while switching child views inside it using `<router-view />`.

Composables: Reusing Logic with the Composition API

With the Composition API, reusable logic lives in **composables**. These are functions that encapsulate a piece of reactive logic you want to share across components.

For example:

```
// composables/useAuth.js
import { computed } from 'vue'
import { useStore } from 'vuex'

export function useAuth() {
  const store = useStore()

  const isLoggedIn = computed(() =>
store.getters['auth/isAuthenticated'])
  const user = computed(() =>
store.state.auth.user)

  const logout = () => {
    store.commit('auth/clearSession')
  }

  return {
    isLoggedIn,
    user,
    logout
  }
}
```

Then in your component:

```
import { useAuth } from '@/composables/useAuth'

const { isLoggedIn, logout } = useAuth()
```

This makes your code more testable, portable, and readable, especially as logic grows in complexity.

API Service Modules

Every feature should have its own service file when consuming APIs. Don't hard-code API calls inside components. Instead, wrap them in dedicated files:

```
// services/userService.js
import api from './api'

export function fetchUserList() {
  return api.get('/users')
}
```

```
export function fetchUserById(id) {
  return api.get(`/users/${id}`)
}
```

Now your component just calls `fetchUserList()` and focuses only on display and interaction.

Planning for Growth

A small app might only need three routes and a single store module. That's fine. But planning a structure that accommodates future growth will save you hours later. A few rules of thumb:

Keep logic modular and reusable

Co-locate related files by feature

Avoid giant, flat folders (e.g., hundreds of files in `components/`)

Document the folder structure for new team members

Separate concerns: views for structure, components for UI, composables for logic, services for data

This mindset helps your Vue project scale without falling apart or becoming painful to refactor later.

Planning the structure of your Vue 3 application is not just about organizing files—it's about building a foundation that can grow with your project. A good structure gives you clarity, consistency, and confidence as you develop more features and bring in more collaborators.

Combining Vuex, Router, and Composition API

In a well-structured Vue 3 application, your state management (Vuex), routing (Vue Router), and logic (Composition API) shouldn't operate in silos—they should work together seamlessly to create a responsive, maintainable experience. Whether you're handling user sessions, navigating between views, or reacting to state changes, the ability to integrate these core systems is what brings your application to life.

Accessing Vuex and Vue Router in a Composition API Component

Vuex and Vue Router both provide special composables in Vue 3:

`useStore()` from `vuex` gives you access to the Vuex store

`useRoute()` and `useRouter()` from `vue-router` let you interact with the current route and programmatic navigation

When you bring all of these into a component using `<script setup>`, the result is a compact but highly readable block of logic.

Practical Scenario: User Profile Component

Your route might look like this:

```
{
  path: '/users/:id',
  name: 'UserProfile',
  component: () =>
import('@/views/users/UserProfileView.vue'),
  meta: { requiresAuth: true }
}
```

Here's what the component might look like using all three tools:

```
<script setup>
import { ref, onMounted } from 'vue'
import { useRoute, useRouter } from 'vue-router'
import { useStore } from 'vuex'
import axios from 'axios'

const route = useRoute()
const router = useRouter()
const store = useStore()

const userId = route.params.id
const user = ref(null)
const loading = ref(true)
const error = ref(null)
```

```
onMounted(async () => {
  try {
    const response = await
axios.get(`/api/users/${userId}`)
    user.value = response.data

    // Set current user globally (for
sidebar/avatar/etc.)
    store.commit('user/setCurrentUser', user.value)
  } catch (err) {
    error.value = 'Failed to load user.'
  } finally {
    loading.value = false
  }
})

const logoutUser = () => {
  store.dispatch('auth/logout')
  router.push('/login')
}
</script>

<template>
  <section v-if="loading">Loading
profile...</section>
  <section v-else-if="error">{{ error }}</section>
  <section v-else>
    <h1>{{ user.name }}</h1>
    <p>{{ user.email }}</p>
    <button @click="logoutUser">Logout</button>
  </section>
</template>
```

Here's what this component is doing:

It reads the route's `:id` param using `useRoute()`

It uses `axios` to fetch data based on the param

It stores the user globally via a Vuex mutation (`user/setCurrentUser`)

It dispatches a logout action via Vuex

It redirects the user using `router.push()` after logout

This illustrates how naturally Vue Router, Vuex, and the Composition API integrate into a single workflow when structured properly.

Handling Protected Routes with Router and Vuex

Many applications have views that require authentication. To enforce this, you can combine Vue Router's `beforeEach()` navigation guard with your Vuex store's authentication state.

In your router configuration:

```
import { createRouter, createWebHistory } from
'vue-router'
import store from '@/store'

const router = createRouter({
  history: createWebHistory(),
  routes: [
    {
      path: '/login',
      name: 'Login',
      component: () =>
import('@/views/auth/LoginView.vue')
    },
    {
      path: '/dashboard',
      name: 'Dashboard',
      component: () =>
import('@/views/dashboard/DashboardHome.vue'),
      meta: { requiresAuth: true }
    }
  ]
})

router.beforeEach((to, from, next) => {
  const isLoggedIn =
store.getters['auth/isAuthenticated']

  if (to.meta.requiresAuth && !isLoggedIn) {
    next('/login')
  } else {
```

```
      next()
   }
})

export default router
```

This checks the `requiresAuth` meta field and reads from the Vuex store to determine if the user is authenticated. You now have centralized, declarative route protection that's tightly coupled with your global state.

Creating a Reusable Composable that Integrates Vuex and Router

You can take commonly used logic and turn it into a **composable** that bridges Vuex and Vue Router.

Let's say you frequently need to check if a user is logged in and redirect if not. Instead of repeating this in multiple components, you can abstract it:

```
// composables/useAuthGuard.js
import { useRouter } from 'vue-router'
import { useStore } from 'vuex'
import { onBeforeMount } from 'vue'

export function useAuthGuard() {
  const store = useStore()
  const router = useRouter()

  onBeforeMount(() => {
    const isLoggedIn =
store.getters['auth/isAuthenticated']
    if (!isLoggedIn) {
      router.push('/login')
    }
  })
}
```

Now in any component:

```
<script setup>
import { useAuthGuard } from
'@/composables/useAuthGuard'
useAuthGuard()
```

```
</script>
```

This allows you to enforce auth on a per-component basis without relying solely on router guards.

Using Vuex and Router in Form Submissions

A common use case is submitting a form, updating the state globally, and redirecting the user—all from the same component.

For instance, a "Create Product" form might look like this:

```
<script setup>
import { ref } from 'vue'
import { useStore } from 'vuex'
import { useRouter } from 'vue-router'

const store = useStore()
const router = useRouter()

const form = ref({
  name: '',
  price: ''
})

const submitting = ref(false)
const error = ref(null)

const submit = async () => {
  submitting.value = true
  error.value = null

  try {
    await store.dispatch('products/createProduct',
form.value)
    router.push('/products')
  } catch (err) {
    error.value = 'Could not create product.'
  } finally {
    submitting.value = false
  }
}
</script>
```

```
<template>
  <form @submit.prevent="submit">
    <input v-model="form.name" placeholder="Name"
/>
    <input v-model="form.price" placeholder="Price"
/>
    <button :disabled="submitting">Create</button>
    <p v-if="error">{{ error }}</p>
  </form>
</template>
```

You're using Vuex to handle the data logic, Vue Router to control navigation, and Composition API to manage state. All three are tightly connected and easy to test independently.

When you combine Vuex, Vue Router, and the Composition API effectively, your Vue 3 application becomes much easier to maintain and scale. Each piece serves its purpose:

Vuex manages shared state across components

Vue Router controls what the user sees and how they get there

The Composition API organizes logic in reusable, readable, testable functions
You've seen how to:
Use Vuex, Router, and Composition API together inside components
Trigger navigations based on actions or auth state
Build reusable logic for auth guards and redirects
Keep components clean by offloading logic into composables and service modules
This integration pattern is what you'll use throughout real-world applications—onboarding flows, dashboards, admin panels, product catalogs, and more.

Authentication and Protected Routes

One of the most critical features in any application that involves users is authentication. Whether you're building a dashboard, an e-commerce backend, a content management system, or anything that requires access control, you'll need a way to identify users, restrict parts of the application to only those who are logged in, and protect routes from unauthorized access.

In a Vue 3 application using the Composition API, Vue Router, and a state management library like Vuex or Pinia, implementing secure and practical authentication flows involves coordinating across multiple layers: storing user session data, intercepting requests to attach tokens, redirecting users when they're not authorized, and updating the UI based on login state.

What Authentication Typically Involves

Authentication typically requires a few coordinated steps:

The user submits login credentials (email/password).

The backend verifies the credentials and returns a signed token (usually a JWT).

The frontend stores the token temporarily (in memory or in `localStorage`).

All future API requests include the token in the `Authorization` header.

The app guards private routes and redirects to login if the user is unauthenticated.

On logout, the token is cleared and the app resets the state.

This is the pattern we'll focus on here, as it's widely compatible with RESTful APIs and microservices.

Building a Login Flow in Vue 3

You'll need a Vuex module (or Pinia store), a login form, and a router configuration that supports protected routes.

Vuex Auth Module Example

```
// store/modules/auth.js
import axios from '@/services/api'

const state = () => ({
  token: null,
  user: null
})
```

```
const getters = {
  isAuthenticated: state => !!state.token,
  currentUser: state => state.user
}

const mutations = {
  setToken(state, token) {
    state.token = token
  },
  setUser(state, user) {
    state.user = user
  },
  clearAuth(state) {
    state.token = null
    state.user = null
  }
}

const actions = {
  async login({ commit }, credentials) {
    const response = await
axios.post('/auth/login', credentials)
    const token = response.data.token
    const user = response.data.user

    localStorage.setItem('auth_token', token)

    commit('setToken', token)
    commit('setUser', user)
  },
  logout({ commit }) {
    localStorage.removeItem('auth_token')
    commit('clearAuth')
  },
  restoreSession({ commit }) {
    const token =
localStorage.getItem('auth_token')
    if (token) {
      commit('setToken', token)
      // Optionally fetch user profile with the
token
```

```
      }
    }
  }

export default {
  namespaced: true,
  state,
  getters,
  mutations,
  actions
}
```

This handles login, logout, and restoring the session from localStorage when the app loads.

Axios Setup to Include Token Automatically

You want all authenticated API requests to automatically include the token.

Here's a reusable Axios instance:

```
// services/api.js
import axios from 'axios'
import store from '@/store'

const api = axios.create({
  baseURL: 'https://api.example.com',
  timeout: 10000
})

api.interceptors.request.use(config => {
  const token = store.state.auth.token
  if (token) {
    config.headers.Authorization = `Bearer ${token}`
  }
  return config
})

export default api
```

With this setup, every time you call `api.get()` or `api.post()`, the token is included if the user is logged in.

Login Component Example

Here's how your login form might look using `<script setup>`:

```
<script setup>
import { ref } from 'vue'
import { useStore } from 'vuex'
import { useRouter } from 'vue-router'

const form = ref({ email: '', password: '' })
const store = useStore()
const router = useRouter()
const error = ref(null)
const loading = ref(false)

const login = async () => {
  loading.value = true
  error.value = null
  try {
    await store.dispatch('auth/login', form.value)
    router.push('/dashboard')
  } catch (err) {
    error.value = 'Invalid email or password.'
  } finally {
    loading.value = false
  }
}
</script>

<template>
  <form @submit.prevent="login">
    <input v-model="form.email" placeholder="Email" />
    <input v-model="form.password" type="password" placeholder="Password" />
    <button :disabled="loading">Login</button>
    <p v-if="error" class="error">{{ error }}</p>
  </form>
</template>
```

This component triggers the Vuex login action, stores the token, and redirects on success. If the login fails, the user sees a meaningful error message.

Protecting Routes with Navigation Guards

Vue Router allows you to guard routes by checking meta fields and the authentication state.

Here's how to enforce that only authenticated users can access certain routes:

```
// router/index.js
import { createRouter, createWebHistory } from
'vue-router'
import store from '@/store'

const routes = [
  {
    path: '/login',
    name: 'Login',
    component: () =>
import('@/views/auth/LoginView.vue')
  },
  {
    path: '/dashboard',
    name: 'Dashboard',
    component: () =>
import('@/views/dashboard/DashboardHome.vue'),
    meta: { requiresAuth: true }
  }
]

const router = createRouter({
  history: createWebHistory(),
  routes
})

router.beforeEach((to, from, next) => {
  const isLoggedIn =
store.getters['auth/isAuthenticated']
  const requiresAuth = to.meta.requiresAuth

  if (requiresAuth && !isLoggedIn) {
    next('/login')
  } else {
    next()
  }
```

```
})

export default router
```

Any route marked with `meta: { requiresAuth: true }` is now protected. If the user isn't logged in, they're redirected to `/login`.

Automatically Restoring Session on App Load

To maintain login across page reloads, restore the session when your app starts. Add this in `main.js`:

```
// main.js
import { createApp } from 'vue'
import App from './App.vue'
import store from './store'
import router from './router'

store.dispatch('auth/restoreSession')

createApp(App)
   .use(store)
   .use(router)
   .mount('#app')
```

Now if a valid token is stored in `localStorage`, the app will recognize the user as logged in when it boots.

Real-World Use Case: Locking the Dashboard

Let's say your application has a sidebar with links to:

/dashboard

/profile

/settings

You only want logged-in users to access these pages. You've already marked them with `meta: { requiresAuth: true }` and your route guard handles redirection.

Now your layout can react to login state like this:

```
<script setup>
import { computed } from 'vue'
import { useStore } from 'vuex'
import { useRouter } from 'vue-router'

const store = useStore()
const router = useRouter()
const isAuthenticated = computed(() =>
store.getters['auth/isAuthenticated'])

const logout = () => {
  store.dispatch('auth/logout')
  router.push('/login')
}
</script>

<template>
  <div>
    <nav v-if="isAuthenticated">
      <router-link
to="/dashboard">Dashboard</router-link>
      <router-link to="/profile">Profile</router-link>
      <router-link to="/settings">Settings</router-link>
      <button @click="logout">Logout</button>
    </nav>
    <router-view />
  </div>
</template>
```

This ensures that your navigation is only available to authenticated users, and clicking "Logout" immediately resets the state and redirects.

Handling authentication and protected routes in a Vue 3 application involves coordination between routing, state management, and secure HTTP requests. When implemented carefully, it creates a seamless experience where users are logged in, remembered, and securely redirected based on their access level.

With this foundation, your application is now secure and session-aware. You can scale it to support user roles, refresh tokens, permissions, and even multi-factor authentication.

Deploying Your App to Netlify, Vercel, or Firebase

Once your Vue 3 application is feature-complete, tested, and ready for users, the next step is getting it out of your development environment and into the hands of real users. Deployment is the process of building your app for production and pushing it to a hosting platform where others can access it over the internet. In the Vue ecosystem, the most seamless way to deploy a frontend SPA (Single Page Application) is through static hosting.

Netlify, Vercel, and Firebase Hosting are three of the most popular platforms for Vue applications today. All three support modern build systems like Vite, offer global CDN delivery, and allow for HTTPS, caching, and custom domain configuration.

Before deploying to any host, your Vue application must be built into static files. If you're using Vite (the recommended tool for Vue 3), this step is simple.

Run the following command:

```
npm run build
```

This creates a `dist/` directory that contains:

An optimized `index.html`

Minified JavaScript and CSS bundles

Static assets (images, fonts, etc.)

Everything needed to serve your app in production

These files are static, meaning they don't require a Node.js server to run. They can be served over any static file host.

Once your app is built, you're ready to deploy it.

Deploying to Netlify

Netlify is one of the most straightforward platforms for deploying Vue applications. It offers continuous deployment from GitHub, drag-and-drop uploads, and intelligent defaults for SPAs.

One-Time Setup

You'll need a Netlify account. You can sign up at https://netlify.com.

Deploy via GitHub

If your code is in a GitHub repository:

Go to the **Netlify Dashboard**.

Click **"Add new site"** → **"Import from Git"**.

Choose GitHub and authorize Netlify if prompted.

Select your Vue repository.

For build settings:

Build command: `npm run build`

Publish directory: `dist`

Click **Deploy Site**.

Netlify will automatically:

Clone your repo

Run your build command

Host your app on a unique Netlify subdomain

Whenever you push updates to the main branch, Netlify will rebuild and redeploy your site.

Handling Vue Router History Mode

If you're using Vue Router in `history` mode (i.e., without hash # in the URLs), you need a `_redirects` file so Netlify knows how to handle routing.

Create this file in your `public/` folder:

```
/*      /index.html    200
```

This tells Netlify to serve `index.html` for all unmatched routes so the Vue router can take over.

Deploying to Vercel

Vercel, created by the team behind Next.js, also offers fast and reliable Vue hosting. It supports auto-deploys from Git, team collaboration, and custom domains.

Deploy from CLI

Install the Vercel CLI:

```
npm i -g vercel
```

From your Vue project root:

```
vercel
```

Follow the prompts:

It will detect a Vite project automatically.

It will ask for the output directory: type `dist`.

Vercel will upload your project and give you a preview link.

Deploy from GitHub

You can also link your GitHub repo:

Go to https://vercel.com.

Click **"New Project"** and select your repository.

Vercel auto-detects Vite and Vue. You can customize build settings if needed.

Click **Deploy**.

As with Netlify, every push to your main branch will trigger a new deploy.

Deploying to Firebase Hosting

Firebase Hosting is another great option, especially if you're using Firebase Auth, Firestore, or Cloud Functions in your project.

Install Firebase CLI

```
npm install -g firebase-tools
```

Login to Firebase

```
firebase login
```

Initialize Firebase in Your Project

From the root of your Vue app:

```
firebase init hosting
```

You'll be asked:

Select a Firebase project → Choose your Firebase project or create one.

Public directory → Enter `dist`

Single-page app? → Yes (this adds the correct rewrite rules)

It will create a `firebase.json` config file and `dist/` will be your deploy target.

Deploy to Firebase

Once your project is built (`npm run build`):

```
firebase deploy
```

Firebase will upload your site, serve it from a global CDN, and give you a live URL.

You can later map a custom domain using the Firebase Console.

Custom Domain Configuration

All three platforms allow you to add a custom domain.

For example, on Netlify:

Go to your site's dashboard.

Click "Domain Settings".

Add your domain (e.g., `example.com`).

Update your DNS provider with the Netlify records provided.

Once the DNS is verified, your app will be live at your domain.

Environment Variables in Production

If your app uses `.env` files for API keys, make sure to set those environment variables in your deployment dashboard.

For example, in Netlify:

Go to "Site Settings" → "Environment Variables"

Add `VITE_API_URL`, `VITE_AUTH_TOKEN`, etc.

Vite exposes these using `import.meta.env.VITE_API_URL`.

Don't forget to **rebuild the app** after changing environment variables.

Once your Vue 3 app is built and tested locally, deployment should not be a bottleneck. With tools like Netlify, Vercel, and Firebase, you can host and deliver your app to users around the world within minutes.

With deployment complete, your app is now accessible to users on the web. From here, you can focus on performance tuning, analytics, security hardening, and monitoring to support your application in the long run.

Performance Optimization and Best Practices

After your Vue 3 application is up and running, the next essential step is ensuring it performs well in real-world conditions. Fast load times, smooth interactivity, and minimal resource usage make the difference between a good user experience and a frustrating one. Even small performance issues can result in high bounce rates, low conversion, or degraded mobile usability.

In production, performance is not just about speed—it's about efficiency, consistency, and making the most of browser resources while respecting your users' devices and network conditions. Optimization doesn't mean rewriting your code from scratch. It's about making deliberate improvements, knowing where bottlenecks can happen, and applying tested techniques to mitigate them.

Lazy Loading Route Components

Vue Router supports route-level code splitting out of the box. This means you don't need to include every view in the initial JavaScript bundle. Instead, Vue can dynamically load components **only when they are needed**.

To apply lazy loading, define routes using dynamic `import()` calls:

```javascript
// router/index.js
import { createRouter, createWebHistory } from
'vue-router'

const routes = [
  {
    path: '/',
    component: () => import('@/views/HomeView.vue')
  },
  {
    path: '/about',
    component: () =>
import('@/views/AboutView.vue')
  },
  {
    path: '/dashboard',
    component: () =>
import('@/views/DashboardView.vue'),
    meta: { requiresAuth: true }
  }
]

const router = createRouter({
  history: createWebHistory(),
  routes
})

export default router
```

Now each view is bundled separately and loaded only when the route is visited. This reduces your initial payload, resulting in faster load times.

Bundle Size Analysis and Optimization

To improve performance, you first need visibility into what's taking up space in your app.

Install and run `rollup-plugin-visualizer` with Vite:

```
npm install --save-dev rollup-plugin-visualizer
```

Then in your `vite.config.js`:

```
import { defineConfig } from 'vite'
import vue from '@vitejs/plugin-vue'
import { visualizer } from 'rollup-plugin-visualizer'

export default defineConfig({
  plugins: [
    vue(),
    visualizer({ open: true })
  ]
})
```

Run:

```
npm run build
```

This will generate an interactive report showing you which libraries and components take up the most space in your final bundle.

From there, you can make informed decisions:

Replace large libraries with lighter alternatives

Tree-shake unused parts of UI libraries

Import only what you use (e.g., importing only icons needed from an icon set)

Efficient Component Design

Components should be as focused and lightweight as possible. A good rule is: **don't make a component do more than it has to**.

For example, if you're displaying a list of users and only showing their name and avatar, don't pass the entire user object:

```
<!-- Avoid this -->
```

```
<UserCard :user="user" />

<!-- Prefer this -->
<UserCard :name="user.name" :avatar="user.avatar"
/>
```

This avoids unnecessary reactivity tracking and improves change detection performance, especially in large lists.

If a component receives a prop that it never actually uses in the template or logic, that's wasted memory and wasted updates.

Avoiding Unnecessary Reactive Overhead

In the Composition API, it's easy to overreactify values. But not everything needs to be reactive.

For example:

```
// Don't wrap constants in ref()
const roles = ['admin', 'editor', 'viewer']
```

Avoid doing this unless you need reactivity:

```
// Only if you need it to change over time
const roles = ref(['admin', 'editor', 'viewer'])
```

Also, if you're working with large objects or arrays that won't change after setup, consider freezing them:

```
const staticOptions = Object.freeze([
  { label: 'Published', value: 'published' },
  { label: 'Draft', value: 'draft' }
])
```

This reduces memory usage and avoids unnecessary tracking by the reactivity system.

Memoization with `computed` and `watch`

Use `computed()` to cache derived data efficiently:

```
const sortedUsers = computed(() => {
```

```
    return [...users.value].sort((a, b) =>
a.name.localeCompare(b.name))
})
```

The sorting logic only re-runs when `users.value` changes—not on every render.

Avoid putting expensive logic inside `watch()` unless you truly need to respond to changes reactively.

Also, be careful with `watchEffect()`—it runs immediately and re-runs every time any dependency changes, which can create unnecessary side effects if used improperly.

Debouncing Input for Expensive Operations

If you're using input to trigger a search or filter operation, debounce it to avoid overloading the system.

Install a debounce utility (like lodash's or your own):

```
npm install lodash.debounce
```

Then:

```
import debounce from 'lodash.debounce'

const searchQuery = ref('')
const debouncedSearch = debounce(async (query) => {
  // trigger API call or filtering
}, 300)

watch(searchQuery, (val) => {
  debouncedSearch(val)
})
```

This ensures the expensive function is only triggered after the user stops typing.

Use Vite's Preloading and Pre-Bundling Features

Vite automatically pre-bundles dependencies for faster dev startup and uses ES modules for production. Still, you can hint the browser to preload key resources.

You can also define asset preload hints in your `index.html`:

```
<link rel="preload"
href="/src/assets/fonts/custom.woff2" as="font"
type="font/woff2" crossorigin="anonymous">
```

This ensures critical assets are fetched earlier in the page load process.

Optimizing Images and Static Assets

Images are often the largest part of a webpage. You can reduce their impact in several ways:

Convert large images to WebP format

Use `srcset` and `<picture>` for responsive image loading

Compress PNG/JPG assets before importing

Use SVGs for icons and logos whenever possible

For example:

```
<picture>
  <source srcset="image.webp" type="image/webp" />
  <img src="image.jpg" alt="Optimized Image" />
</picture>
```

This gives modern browsers the optimized version and falls back to the standard one.

Avoid Global Event Listeners in Components

Avoid setting up global listeners (`window`, `document`, etc.) in components unless necessary. If you must use them, clean up manually:

```
onMounted(() => {
  window.addEventListener('resize', handleResize)
})

onBeforeUnmount(() => {
```

```
    window.removeEventListener('resize',
handleResize)
})
```

Not cleaning up will lead to memory leaks and degraded performance over time, especially in single-page apps where components are reused frequently.

Prefetching Routes and Code Splits

Vue Router supports route prefetching. You can hint at which routes should be loaded early (e.g., dashboard after login).

With `<router-link>`, use:

```
<router-link to="/dashboard" v-slot="{ href, route,
navigate, isActive, isExactActive }">
  <a :href="href"
@mouseenter="navigate">Dashboard</a>
</router-link>
```

This starts loading the chunk on mouseover instead of click, improving perceived performance.

Monitoring and Continuous Testing

Finally, performance isn't a one-time optimization—it should be part of your development and deployment process.

Use tools like:

Lighthouse (available in Chrome DevTools or CI) to measure performance, accessibility, and SEO

WebPageTest for real-world network performance

Sentry or **LogRocket** for error tracking and performance analytics in production

Set up performance budgets so you get alerts if your JS bundle or image assets grow beyond limits you've defined.

Optimizing a Vue 3 application requires deliberate choices across all layers of your app—from the way you split code, structure components, manage state, load images, and even respond to user interactions.

Appendices

The appendices are included to provide extended, reference-focused material for readers who want to deepen their understanding, avoid common mistakes, and explore Vue's evolving ecosystem. While the main chapters focus on building applications and learning patterns in a guided manner, these additional sections offer quick-access information, insights into best practices, and optional yet practical knowledge areas such as testing and migration.

A. Vue 3 Composition API Reference

The Composition API introduced in Vue 3 gives developers a flexible and powerful way to organize logic within components. Instead of relying on the Options API structure (`data`, `methods`, `computed`, etc.), the Composition API allows you to define state, functions, and reactive behavior using imported functions in a unified `setup()` block.

At the center of the Composition API are several key functions:

`ref()` is used to create a reactive primitive. You can wrap strings, numbers, booleans, or even objects with it, and it will return a reactive reference that you can track and bind in your template. To access the actual value in JavaScript, use `.value`.

`reactive()` creates a deeply reactive object or array. Unlike `ref()`, you don't need to use `.value` when accessing its properties, but changes are still reactive.

`computed()` returns a read-only derived value. It automatically recalculates when any of its dependencies change. Useful for deriving values from reactive state.

`watch()` allows you to run side effects when a specific reactive source changes. It can track single or multiple sources and respond to deep changes if needed.

`watchEffect()` is similar to `watch()` but runs immediately and automatically tracks any reactive values accessed during execution.

`onMounted()`, `onUnmounted()`, `onUpdated()` and other lifecycle hooks are functions that allow you to hook into the component's lifecycle while using the Composition API.

Together, these functions allow you to structure reusable logic that's clean, modular, and easy to reason about across large applications.

B. Common Patterns and Anti-Patterns

Writing Vue 3 applications that are easy to maintain comes down to using patterns that support clarity, testability, and reusability. At the same time, it's important to identify anti-patterns that can lead to bugs or complexity.

One helpful pattern is the use of composables. A composable is simply a function that encapsulates reactive state and related logic using the Composition API. This makes it easier to reuse logic across multiple components without repeating code or creating tightly coupled dependencies.

Another good pattern is keeping your component logic focused. Each component should have a single responsibility—whether that's rendering a list, managing a form, or handling layout. When components grow too large, it becomes harder to reason about how and why they update.

Anti-patterns often stem from misuse of reactivity. Wrapping everything in `ref()` or `reactive()` without clear intent can cause unnecessary updates or make debugging difficult. Similarly, directly mutating props inside child components goes against Vue's unidirectional data flow and should be avoided. Instead, use `emit()` to communicate changes back to the parent.

Overusing global state is another common mistake. Not everything belongs in Vuex or a global store. Local state should stay in the component where it's used unless it's needed elsewhere.

Finally, avoid logic in templates. Computation, filtering, and manipulation should be handled in the `setup()` function or computed properties—not inline inside the template markup.

C. Testing Vue Apps (Optional Reading)

Testing isn't mandatory for small projects, but it becomes invaluable as applications grow. With Vue 3, you can write both unit tests and integration tests using tools like Vitest, Jest, and Vue Test Utils.

Unit tests focus on testing individual pieces of logic in isolation. These are ideal for testing composables, store actions, or utility functions. You provide inputs and verify that the outputs are correct.

Component tests focus on rendering Vue components and checking their behavior. You can simulate user interaction, assert that reactive state updates correctly, and confirm that emitted events occur as expected.

End-to-end testing, using tools like Cypress or Playwright, simulates actual user behavior in the browser. These tests cover navigation, form submissions, routing guards, and visual regressions.

Using mocks and stubs helps isolate what you're testing. For example, when testing a component that uses an API call, you might mock the service call and return a static response instead of hitting a real backend.

While writing tests adds time upfront, it dramatically reduces the chances of regressions and makes refactoring safer over time.

D. Migration Tips from Vue 2 to Vue 3

Vue 3 introduces significant improvements in performance, reactivity, and developer experience. However, migrating from Vue 2 to Vue 3 can involve breaking changes, especially if you rely on plugins or the Options API in a specific way.

The first step is to upgrade all third-party dependencies and ensure they are compatible with Vue 3. Libraries like Vue Router and Vuex have Vue 3 versions, but older versions won't work with the new reactivity system.

The Composition API is optional—you can use the Options API in Vue 3. That said, many developers gradually migrate parts of their app to the Composition API as they refactor. You don't need to rewrite everything immediately.

Use the official migration build (`@vue/compat`) if you need to transition incrementally. It allows Vue 3 to run Vue 2-style code with warnings about deprecated usage. This is helpful for large applications that can't migrate all at once.

Watch out for removed APIs like `filters`, and changes to how `v-model` and event modifiers behave. Also, Vue 3 uses proxies for reactivity, which changes how objects and arrays are tracked internally.

Lastly, tools like the Vue Migration Guide and the Vue CLI upgrade helper can automate some of the refactoring and warn you about potential issues.

E. Recommended Tools and Ecosystem Libraries

The Vue ecosystem is rich with tools that help you build faster, scale better, and stay productive. Whether you're handling state, forms, styling, or testing, there are libraries that integrate cleanly with Vue 3.

For state management, Vuex is still widely used, but Pinia is now the officially recommended alternative. It provides a simpler, more intuitive API and better TypeScript support out of the box.

For routing, Vue Router remains the official solution and supports all of Vue 3's features, including composition-friendly hooks like `useRoute()` and `useRouter()`.

For forms and validation, libraries like VeeValidate, Vuelidate, and Yup (in combination with your own form logic) give you structure and validation capabilities. They're useful in complex forms with dynamic fields or custom error handling.

When working with APIs, Axios remains the most popular HTTP client, but you can also consider GraphQL clients like `graphql-request` or Apollo Client if you're using a GraphQL backend.

For styling, many teams use Tailwind CSS due to its utility-first approach and excellent support in Vue projects. You can also use Sass, PostCSS, or component libraries like Vuetify, Quasar, and Element Plus depending on your design goals.

On the tooling side, Vite has become the de facto standard build tool for Vue 3 apps. It's fast, lightweight, and works seamlessly with Vue Single File Components.

If you're building static sites or content-driven apps, Nuxt 3 builds on top of Vue 3 and provides server-side rendering, routing, and a plugin system for larger projects.

Each of these tools has strengths in different situations. The key is to choose based on your needs—performance, flexibility, or development speed—and keep your stack as lean as possible.